6

D1274144

Ms.—Attorney

by D. X. Fenten

THE WESTMINSTER PRESS
PHILADELPHIA

PUBLISHED BY THE WESTMINSTER PRESS ®
PHILADELPHIA, PENNSYLVANIA

PRINTED IN THE UNITED STATES OF AMERICA

5   4   3   2

Library of Congress Cataloging in Publication Data

Fenten, D. X.
    Ms.—attorney.

    SUMMARY: Discusses, for women interested in a law career, the scholastic preparation necessary, the training required for different specialties, and the particular challenges they face as women.
    1. Women lawyers—United States.   2. Law—Study and teaching—United States.   3. Law schools—United States —Directories.   [1. Law as a profession.   2. Women lawyers.   3. Law—Study and teaching.   4. Law schools] I. Title.
KF299.W6F45   340'.023   74–4492
ISBN 0–664–32552–1

Contents

Preface

That God designed the sexes to occupy different spheres
of action, and that it belongs to men to make, apply and
execute the laws, was regarded as an almost axiomatic
truth. . . . We are certainly warranted in saying that
when the Legislature gave to this court the power of
granting licenses to practice law, it was not with the
slightest expectation that this privilege would be ex-
tended equally to men and women. . . . It is not merely
an immense innovation in our own usages as a court
that we are asked to make. This step, if taken by us,
would mean that in the opinion of this tribunal, every
civil office in this State may be filled by women—that it
is in harmony with the spirit of our Constitution and
laws that women should be made governors, judges and
sheriffs. This we are not yet prepared to hold.

With these and a few more well-chosen words, the
application of one of the first women to attempt to
practice law in the United States was denied by the
Illinois Supreme Court. That was in 1870, a bit over one
century ago.

Have times changed? Are women now welcomed with open arms into law schools, law practices, the courts, and elective and appointive offices? If the answers to these questions were "Yes," or even a qualified "Yes, but . . . ," there would be far less need for this book.

Most Americans have been conditioned by habit to expect male lawyers, male judges, and male politicians. They believe, as did the Wisconsin Supreme Court in 1875, that

> Nature has tempered woman as little for the judicial conflicts of the courtroom as for the physical conflicts of the battlefield. Woman is modeled for gentler and better things. It . . . [the law profession] . . . has essentially and habitually to do with all that is selfish and extortionate, knavish and criminal, coarse and brutal, repulsive and obscene in human life. It would be revolting to all female sense of innocence and sanctity of their sex, shocking to man's reverence for woman- hood and faith in woman on which hinge all the better affections and humanities of life, that woman should be permitted to mix professionally in all the nastiness of the world which finds its way into the courts of justice. . . . Discussions are habitually necessary which are unfit for female ears. The habitual presence of women at these would tend to relax the public sense of decency and propriety.

The road to a rewarding career in law is long and difficult for men. It is many times more difficult for women. That is the reason for this book. We need more women lawyers, not because they are women, but because they would make fine lawyers. Too many very well qualified women college graduates are "turned off" from law as a profession because it is now and has always been considered a "masculine profession."

We will examine the facts of the situation in this book, not through the rose-colored glasses of recruitment, but through the magnifying glass of reality. We hope these facts will not deter but instead will cause many young women actively to seek careers in the law.

This book was written during the Senate Watergate Hearings. During these hearings the feelings toward lawyers and the profession of law were at a very low point. Almost all the defendants were practicing lawyers and, supposedly, the best there were.

At this time one would have expected that *all* lawyers would be especially sensitive to the feelings of people toward their profession and would "bend over backward" to try to establish even slightly better public relations.

Surprisingly that was not the case. Not only did the lawyers, law firms, and law schools that we contacted not "bend over backward" in assisting in the preparation of this book, they were almost to a man uncooperative, disinterested, and frequently rude. In seventeen previous nonfiction books, this is the first time that this has ever happened. In all other cases the subjects of my books have been enthusiastic, extremely helpful, encouraging, and fully cooperative.

For this reason and for the many reasons developed throughout this book, I am convinced that male lawyers do not want a book to encourage women to enter law, nor do they want women lawyers at all. The question comes to mind: Are the male lawyers afraid to share a good thing, or are they fearful that young, energetic, idealistic women who have worked hard to get into the profession will "make waves" once they are in it?

Fortunately, some people did help with the information-gathering and the writing of this book. To name them all would add little. Instead, the author gratefully acknowledges the assistance of lawyers, judges, professors—women and men from all over the United States who "could find the time." Special thanks go to the legal societies and associations for whatever help they could provide.

You will note that there are neither legal citations nor bibliographical references for quoted material. All the material used in this book is from recognized leaders, women and men, in the legal profession. Citing the sources would have added little to the validity of the quotations and much to the weight of the book.

Once again, very special thanks goes to my "home team" without whom none of my books would have been possible. To my parents, my wife, and my children go my heartfelt thanks for their help, their encouragement, their love, and for their very tangible support in editing, typing, and proofreading.

D.X.F.

Greenlawn, New York

1
Just Call Her "Esquire"

Sound: (Baby crying)

Announcer: This healthy, normal baby has a handicap. She was born female. When she grows up, her job opportunities will be limited, and her pay low. As a sales clerk, for instance, she'll earn half of what a man does. If she goes to college, she'll still earn less than many men with an eighth grade education. In a democracy, equal pay and equal opportunities for women should be a goal we all wish to achieve. Job discrimination based on sex is against the law. And it's a waste. Think about your own daughter—she's handicapped too.

Womanpower. It's Much Too Good to Waste.

That's the way the National Organization of Women (NOW) tells Americans over radio and television about the absurdity of job discrimination. Is this kind of story really true? Are women discriminated against when they try to get good jobs? Equal pay for equal work? Promotions and status? Are we wasting a lot of talent and ability by making women second-class citizens? Yes! Yes! Yes!

How about careers in law? Can women get into the "good" law schools? And, once they have law degrees, can women achieve satisfying careers in the legal profession? Can they practice in all the legal "specialities" or are they limited to certain areas such as domestic relations law or juvenile work because of their "alleged" special sensitivity or concern with people?

There is no question about discrimination against women in the legal profession. It has existed and still exists today, effectively keeping the practice of law a man's world. After a "bumper" crop of female lawyers from law school, *The New York Times* reported in December 1972 that "women lawyers were *boosted* to a *meager* 4.6% of the profession by this year's graduates."

A considerable part of the problem is rooted deeply in the traditional view of women. It was stated quite clearly by the United States Supreme Court in 1872 upholding a state law barring women from the practice of law: "Man is, or should be, woman's protector and defender. The natural and proper timidity and delicacy which belongs to the female sex evidently unfits it for many of the occupations of civil life." Many years later, noted lawyer Clarence Darrow was quoted as adding insult to injury by saying:

> You can't be shining lights at the bar because you are too kind. You can never be corporation lawyers because you are not cold blooded.
>
> You have not a high grade of intellect.

This healthy, normal baby has a handicap. She was born female.

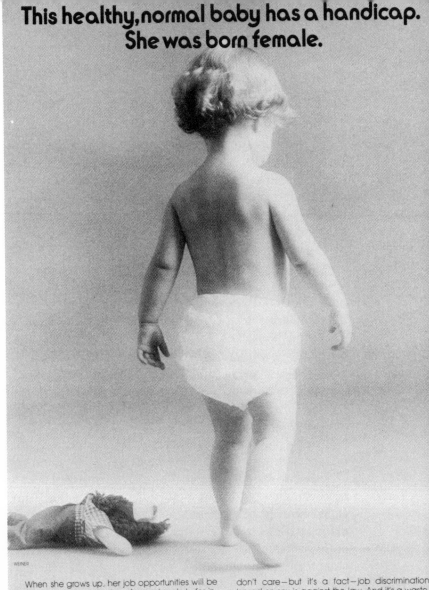

When she grows up, her job opportunities will be limited, and her pay low. As a sales clerk, for instance, she'll earn half of what a man does. If she goes to college, she'll still earn less than many men with a 9th grade education. Maybe you don't care—but it's a fact—job discrimination based on sex is against the law. And it's a waste. Think about your own daughter—she's handicapped too.

Womanpower. It's much too good to waste.

This advertisement prepared for Ms. magazine by volunteers through de Garmo, Inc. for the National Organization for Women.

National Organization for Women

This advertisement appeared as a public service in major American newspapers and magazines to draw attention to pervasive bias

You can never expect to get the fees men get. I doubt if you even make a living.

All this bias does not start with a woman's application to a law school or with her application for a job with a law firm. It starts much, much earlier. Matter of fact, it starts when she is a very little girl. Her female handicap is nurtured all the while she is being raised. In a companion book in this series, *Ms.—M.D.*, a leading male psychiatrist spelled out this handicap:

"Once a child's biological identity is settled, the female child is generally handled more gently than the male child and addressed in softer tones. She is given different toys to play with—dolls, kitchen utensils, miniature household furniture, sewing kits. The little boy is given war games, tools, athletic equipment. Boys and girls are given different chores to do; girls are expected to help with inside matters—the dishes, dusting the furniture, etc.; boys with outside matters—raking leaves, shoveling snow, etc.

"Above all, however, boys and girls, from earliest life on, are confronted with *differing expectations.* Girls are expected to be coquettish, submissive, and dependent; boys to be aggressive and independent. Girls are expected to be competent about household matters and in fine arts but to be relatively helpless and incompetent in most 'practical' matters. Boys are expected to be competent in mathematics, manual crafts, science, and worldly affairs. Most importantly, girls are raised with the expectation that their primary goal in life is to get married and have children while boys are taught that their primary goal is to have some sort of work career, with marriage and fatherhood as a secondary goal. Moreover, boys are expected—even pressured—to go to college and graduate school; girls are not expected to, to the same extent, and indeed are often overtly or covertly discouraged from doing so. This takes place not only within the home but also in the crucial high school years where girls are usually not encouraged toward the field of mathematics or science and are often subtly guided toward more 'feminine' aspirations."

O.K. You're a big girl now. You know the problem and understand about your "handicap." You know you must be realistic. What chance do you have of making it? Of getting into law school? Of getting a good job? Of having a successful, rewarding career in law?

One woman lawyer, who has been practicing for more than forty years, summarized the answers to all these questions by saying, "For a woman to make it as a lawyer she's got to be a fighter. She's got to be self-confident, have very broad shoulders and, most of all, she's got to have guts. If these characteristics are not part of her makeup, she's better off in another field."

According to current American Bar Association (ABA) statistics, there are more women attending law schools today than ever before. That statistic sounds good, and that's part of the problem—it sounds a lot better than it really is. Female enrollment in law schools had no place to go but up. And though the number of women law students is definitely increasing, the numbers are not even close to being proportionate with the number of male college graduates who seek admission.

Changes have been and continue to be made. Just about all the barriers to the admission of females to law school have been removed. Some law schools had their own sex antidiscrimination policies in effect for a long time before these policies became the law for all. In December 1970 all member schools of the Association of American Law Schools (AALS) adopted equality of opportunity standards which stated: "To the end that high standards of legal education be fostered, each member school shall maintain: Equality of opportunity in legal education without discrimination or segregation on the ground of race, color, religion, national origin, or sex."

All of this did not cause a sudden rush either of women to law schools or of law schools to look for likely women candidates. The fact remains that there are far fewer seats available in this country's law schools than there are bodies who want to fill them. Part of the change that has occurred has been that many law schools, including the most prestigious, are now actively trying to bring the proportion of men and women students more into line. One admissions officer candidly admits that he tends, "all things being equal, to favor women applicants over men, if for no other reason than to help right the existing imbalance in the makeup of the legal profession."

A few prestige law schools are making special efforts to recruit women at the women's colleges and to explain the reasons why they should study law. Duke University tries to encourage women to seek admission with a specially designed brochure that asks the question: "Is Law School any place for a woman?" They answer: "The Duke University Law School thinks so." Another school, Rutgers, took additional positive action when it approved the following guidelines:

> Female gender is a favorable factor. Discrimination based on sex is unlawful and unwanted. The facts indicate that the number of women applicants is increasing rapidly and that larger numbers of women will be accepted without any dilution of academic standards. Active recruitment of women as applicants is desirable. In view of the difficulties to which women have been subjected in the recent past when they sought to enter the legal profession, it appears appropriate, for the immediate short-term future, to consider the female gender as a favorable factor where choices need to be made among applicants who are approximately equal in other respects. Such a policy ought to be applied moderately and be subject to continued review.

What has all this actually meant to women who want to go to law school and to women already in law school? The Women's Law Association of Harvard University reports:

> There have been victories at the law school, not without significance in the broader context of women's relationship to Harvard University. The real Victory, of course, will take place within people's heads.

> • The admissions office and admissions committee have been made fully aware of women's concern with this area of law school policy. Women students have been given funds for a limited fall recruitment effort. We have also been supported in principle: there should be more women at HLS, and more women should be encouraged to apply.

• The placement office has instituted procedures to investigate and act upon charges of discrimination in hiring by those who use its facilities. If employers are found to have violated Harvard's strong policy of nondiscrimination, they are barred from interviewing at the law school.

• Hastings Hall, the poshest of the law school's dormitories, has had women residents since 1970.

• One law school professor deliberately excised all sexism from his casebook on commercial transactions.

• Part of a law school building was made available, without charge, for a day-care center which opened in September, 1971, for children of HLS students, faculty, and staff.

• Cheap shots at women have all but disappeared from their traditional niches in torts and criminal law classes.

• A gynecologist has been added to the staff of the University Health Services.

• The Women's Law Association has its own office.

• A credit course on Women and the Law is in its second year.

Though it would seem that progress is being made toward getting more qualified women into and through law school, all is not yet "peaches and cream." Many old-line males still give women a very hard time, whenever and wherever they can. For example, a first-year law student wrote to an eminent lawyer:

At the preliminary screening interview one of the professors stated point blank that he could not see why

Progress is being made toward equality for women in law school. In this "moot court" at New York University women are pictured in both prosecution and defense positions

women were being admitted into the law school when they were merely taking up places men could be sitting in. And he proceeded to give me the "typical" male argument about how when a woman gets married and bears children, she concludes her legal career.

I naturally defended the right of women in law school. He answered by telling me of a woman doctor friend who has "wasted" her medical education by giving it up for being a housewife and a mother.

Other law students report continually disparaging remarks about women, especially women law students, by professors in the classroom. One recent law school graduate tells the story of a professor whose approach to women law students is to call on them on one designated day (Ladies Day) during the semester and then ignore them the remainder of the time. When the students complained to him about this practice and asked whether he would also have a special Blacks Day, Jews Day, or Catholics Day, he is reported to have said, "Of course not, that would be discriminatory."

Despite what appears to be common practice in many law schools—professors not calling on women students in class—women students are usually treated pretty much the way other students are treated. As a matter of fact, some women students even report a difference and a deference in the attitude of certain professors toward them and feel that this treatment is not to their detriment.

If discrimination is indeed diminishing for a woman seeking to enter law school and if it is not really a "major problem" while she is a student, it is a far different story when she tries to enter the legal profession itself. Most female attorneys agree that their most serious setbacks come when they set out to get their *first* jobs. Employers (especially the lawyers and law firms who might hire a newly graduated lawyer) have many doubts about hiring new female lawyers.

They doubt a woman lawyer's "willingness to behave herself in a predominantly male setting." They doubt that a woman lawyer is a good career risk because they assume she will give up her career for marriage or childbearing ("no woman will continue her career [for] long after marriage or pregnancy, so why bother hiring her?"). They doubt that a female is as good a lawyer as is a man "because female lawyers are intellectually inferior and more prone to emotional reasoning than male attorneys." They doubt that their clients would accept working with a female lawyer and "might resent having their case 'palmed off' on a woman attorney." This would indicate to the client that the firm considers the matter too insignificant to warrant the superior services of a male member of the staff. They also doubt that women will stay in one place, with one firm very long, because "women will always give up their jobs to allow their husbands to move to a different area so the men can get a better position and further the husband's career."

The list of "doubts" goes on and on. Most of these myths are contradicted by common sense, the remainder by statistics. Recent studies by both Columbia and Harvard Universities reveal that women *do* proceed to practice law and don't give it up for good when they get married or have children. Harvard found that of its female law school graduates, 84 percent still practice law. The remaining 16 percent plan to return to practice when their children have grown past infancy. So female lawyers do not desert career and employer for husband and child. In fact, many female lawyers are married to lawyers. The studies showed that Harvard Law School women graduates married lawyers 63 percent of the time and female Columbia School of Law graduates married lawyers 60 percent of the time. These people are not about to give up careers and employers whenever their spouses are offered greener pastures elsewhere.

While Title VII of the Civil Rights Act of 1964 declared a national policy against job discrimination because of sex, it appears that lawyers can give all kinds of advice on the law to their clients without considering it for themselves.

A typical job-hunting situation is graphically described by a female Harvard Law School graduate in part in a letter to the *Harvard Law Record*:

> The point of this letter is not to go into my work experience with the one firm that finally did offer me a job. What I wanted to write about is those awful, funny, sad interviews, because your article indicates not much has changed in three years. First of all, some of the firms I signed up to see didn't even schedule me for an interview. I don't know if they really did talk *only* to *Law Review* students, as was rumored, or if they just weren't interested in another woman for their ghetto. If the latter was their reason, they were among the most honest firms on the Boston list, and they didn't waste any of my time for which I was grateful.

I still have my interview cards; there are sixteen of them, unless I have lost a few. Looking through them, I see a succession of similar interviews, very dull and very quick, in which I made a few notes on what the firm did with new associates, which was my prime question. I had begun to sense that the areas of law for women in Boston were: probate of estates, estate planning, real estate, and maybe some tax, and it really would not be difficult at all to get a job at a spiffy firm, if I would just say I would work *only* in one of those areas; or if I would say I would do *nothing* but research in their library. But I had made up my mind I wouldn't take that route, unless I absolutely had to.

It appears from the interview cards that the interviews were twenty minutes each. I remember that I was usually ushered in *at least* five or ten minutes late, but that I was always ushered out exactly on time. I must have been a pleasant coffee break for them, after that first crucial question was asked ("Would you be at all interested in working in estate planning?"), and thereafter they seemed to be rehearsing their spiel about their firm on me.

The unusual ones stand out. One interviewer had me in and out of the office in less than five minutes! The only notation I made on the card was that his firm had hired their first woman the year before. ("We have our one woman, one Jew, one Negro. . . .")

And there was the guy who was cruelly honest. As soon as I walked into the room he said he didn't want to waste my time, but the chances of his firm's hiring me were zero. It seems they had had a lady lawyer once, and it didn't work out at all because the secretaries didn't like her. And even though it was too bad that she

was such a sour apple—a woman lawyer? *never* again!
He was very pleasant, and said I could stay and talk to
him for the remaining fifteen minutes if I wanted. Why
didn't I leave, and scream at the Placement Office
director and tell her that such firms should be *made* to
put "No women need apply" on their interview sheets,
and stop wasting my time by scheduling phoney interviews with me? . . .

I finally blew my cool in one interview. It was scheduled
for 5:00 P.M., and my usual practice was to go home
after morning classes, but I had wandered around the
law school this long afternoon waiting for this one five
o'clock interview, and I went in and two very nice
interviewers, who were also tired, began by getting to
the point and asking me if I would be at all interested in
doing estate work, and I said no, and they were eager to
call it a day and get out, but somehow they were
compelled to explain their haste, so they said they
weren't against hiring a woman as a general associate
themselves, but that their clients wouldn't like it and
they had to think of their business. From somewhere I
let loose a tirade of words about how they substitute
"black" for "woman" in everything they were saying
and it would make as much "practical" sense, but they
would be very embarrassed for having said it, for the
country now recognized such prejudice against blacks
as immoral and most educated people would be embarrassed to admit to it so blatantly. And I said that their
arguments, or excuses, were just plain immoral. (Unfortunately I didn't know enough to say "against the
law of the land, you officers of the court.") And you
know, the funny thing is that they just sat there and
took it. When I was done, they *agreed* with me. And the
only way they could find to end the interview was to say

that it certainly had been interesting talking to me. I want to give the correct impression of this interview. I do *not* feel these men were patronizing me or just letting me blow off steam. I felt like I really was communicating with them, and yet they, competent, practicing lawyers, could offer *no* rebuttal to my arguments. The only explanation I can find for that is that they appreciated that their views were indefensible.

Lawyers are not the only ones to blame for the disgraceful discrimination against women lawyers. We all are. We have gotten so accustomed to the idea that the male is superior that we want our doctors, lawyers, and everyone else important to be men. Even women discriminate against women.

That is the picture, and it's not a pretty one. Discrimination against women lawyers is a fact of life in the legal profession in America. It is getting better, but not nearly fast enough.

Now, how about you? Does this appalling picture turn you off? Are you ready to look for a different career? Going to give up your dream of law? If you answer yes, then you're right and the law is not for you. If, however, what you have read has raised your blood pressure and made you "spitting mad"—wonderful. You've got spunk. You've got guts. You've got what it takes to go out after what you want. You have the basic requirements to make it as a woman lawyer. If you need any further reassurance, think of the words of a famous judge who said, "It is surely not without significance that the age-old symbol of Justice is a woman."

2
Portia and Others Face Life

We haven't always had laws, at least not the way we know them today. We've had folkways, customs, taboos. Until relatively recently laws were strong but informal, overwhelming but unwritten. For a very long time man's life and the way he lived that life was governed by the experiences of his father and his father's father. He didn't need our kind of laws, he just followed the customs and folkways that were handed down to him and would be handed down to his children.

In all of this, down through the ages, women have had little part. There are frequent customs and taboos concerning women, but always of a very practical nature and always as it affected that "superior being," the man. There was a lot of fear, superstition and, later, religion built into these customs and folkways. As a result, primitive people lived carefully and were relatively well behaved. But who wouldn't be, knowing that breaking a taboo meant facing the tribal elders, the fierce medicine man or one of any number of terrifying gods! Until this point there was no need for written laws. It was quite enough to pass the taboos and customs down from one generation to the next.

As primitive societies became more sophisticated, larger, and better organized, more and more "laws" were developed. They came out of everyday dealings and situations, but they started to pile up. Now, in addition to the governing of one person's life and that of his family, there was a need to govern commerce and the way people dealt with other people. In time, the customs, taboos, and folkways became so numerous and so involved that it was virtually impossible to remember them all. It was then time to start writing them down, to separate realistic rules from magic, superstition, and taboo: to make a set of rules that would serve as the basic law of the land.

Each important civilization survives in our lives today through the laws and the influence of lawgivers. One of the earliest legal codes preserved to this day came from Hammurabi, who ruled in Babylonia some thirty-eight hundred years ago. Based on older collections of laws that Hammurabi revised, adjusted, and expanded, the code of Hammurabi covered such matters as false accusation, witchcraft, military service, land and business regulations, family laws, tariffs, wages, trade, loans and debts. From this code came the principle "The strong shall not injure the weak," and punishment for crimes—literally, "an eye for an eye."

Some seven hundred years later, around 1200 B.C., Moses gave the Hebrews and the world the Ten Commandments and the remainder of the law in the

Pentateuch or Torah. Whether or not he wrote the laws or merely reported what God had given him is not nearly so important as the laws themselves, which are to be found in one form or another in the laws of all peoples throughout history. The woman's role, which has persisted down through the ages, is spelled out in the Bible, in God's words to Eve (as punishment for having disobeyed him): "I will greatly multiply thy sorrow and thy conception; in sorrow shalt thou bring forth children; and thy desire shall be to thy husband, and he shall rule over thee."

The Greeks made a major change in the concept of law and legal affairs. Before the Greeks, people believed that laws came from a god or a group of gods. The Greeks introduced the idea that laws were made by men and because of this could be changed by men whenever the need arose. The Greeks respected the law more than any people before them and respected those men who drew up and administered the laws. One of these men, Solon, was chief magistrate of Athens about 594 B.C. His contributions were many and important, and included the modification of laws requiring the death penalty for most offenses and the recognition of all citizen's rights to similar treatment under the law and in voting. He managed to alienate Athenian women with some of his "reforms," including the legalization of prostitution and also the requirement that a bride bring with her no more than three changes of clothing. But he also gave women some social protection by providing that a daughter or sister could not be sold into slavery unless she were an "unmarried wanton," and he set new fines for rape and seduction (unless the woman was a harlot).

The Romans are credited with the establishment of the beginnings of the legal profession and the legalization of a fee for a lawyer's services. Many legal innovations came out of the years of the Roman Empire, including the codification of all Roman laws by the Emperor Justinian. All of this had considerable influence on later civilizations and on lawgivers throughout the world.

A woman did not have many legal rights under the Roman laws, and, interestingly, her life was quite similar to that of the American woman of not so long ago. In ancient Rome women were under "perpetual tutelage"—while at home a girl was under her father's control. To get out of her father's control she married, but all that this did was to pass control either to her husband or to her husband's father. She had not much in the way of emancipation in Rome—or anywhere else, for that matter.

And there certainly wasn't much emancipation in the American colonies many hundreds of years later. In fact the law itself, as a profession, was in pretty sad shape. Deeply suspicious of English common law because of its harsh punishments for dissenters, colonists envisioned a "wonderful new society without lawyers." Puritans considered the practice of law "a dark and knavish business" and required no lawyer for litigation, only a magistrate, and he needed to know no law. Justice was dispensed according to the Bible and a few local ordinances; judges were not even required to be men of the bar. Historical research reveals that as late as 1698 lawyers were classed in one Connecticut law along with "drunkards and keepers of disorderly houses"; that until 1712 in Massachusetts and 1754 in

New Hampshire the chief justice was not a lawyer. "One reason the law was in such a bad state was that there were so few lawyers, and one reason there were so few lawyers was that the laws were in such a bad state."

Soon, however, despite a "profound distrust" of professional lawyers, the need for them in the emerging society was felt. A number of lawyers, many trained at the Inns of Court in England, tried to correct the abuses facing the colonists. Several became political leaders in a time when leadership was at a low ebb. Of the fifty-six signers of the Declaration of Independence, twenty-five were lawyers.

But independence, emancipation, and freedom for women were still a long way off. The new nation that spoke of freedom for its people had only men in mind—and white men at that. For everyone else there was still a long, long way to go for any kind of independence.

In 1869, British philosopher, John Stuart Mill, wrote about "the dull and hopeless life" of women in an essay on *The Subjection of Women.* In part he said:

> There is no country of Europe in which the ablest men have not frequently experienced, and keenly appreciated, the value of the advice and help of clever and experienced women of the world, in the attainment both of private and of public objects; and there are important matters of public administration to which few men are equally competent with such women; among others, the detailed control of expenditure. But what we are now discussing is not the need which society has of the services of women in public business, but the dull and hopeless life to which it so often condemns them, by

forbidding them to exercise the practical abilities which many of them are conscious of, in any wider field than one which to some of them never was, and to others is no longer, open. If there is anything vitally important to the happiness of human beings, it is that they should relish their habitual pursuit. This requisite of an enjoyable life is very imperfectly granted, or altogether denied, to a large part of mankind; and by its absence many a life is a failure, which is provided, in appearance, with every requisite of success.

What in unenlightened societies color, race, religion, or in the case of a conquered country, nationality, are to some men, sex is to all women; a peremptory exclusion from almost all honorable occupations, but either such as cannot be fulfilled by others, or such as those others do not think worthy of their acceptance. Sufferings arising from causes of this nature usually meet with so little sympathy that few persons are aware of the great amount of unhappiness even now produced by the feeling of a wasted life. The case will be even more frequent, as increased cultivation creates a greater and greater disproportion between the ideas and faculties of women, and the scope which society allows to their activity.

It was just this, "the scope which society allows for their activity," that finally got this country its first female lawyer. In June 1869, in Mount Pleasant, Iowa, Arabella A. Mansfield (Mrs. Belle A. Mansfield was the name she was more frequently called) was admitted to the bar of the State of Iowa. That was a wonderful year for women in America, for, in addition to Mrs. Mansfield's triumph, there were several more. In this same year women matriculated for the first time in St. Louis

Law School, the first law school in the country where a
law degree was awarded regardless of sex. And also in
1869 women first won the right to vote, though it was
only in territorial elections in the Wyoming and Mor-
mon territories.

As was the practice for many men at that time, Belle
Mansfield studied law in a law office and at home, not
in a law school. Her studies completed, she applied for
admission to the bar. For a woman to be admitted to
the bar at that time required a state court decision or an
act of the legislature or both. It would be wonderful to
be able to report that Mrs. Mansfield gained admission
strictly on her merit as a lawyer. Such was not the case.
The Iowa code in force at that time limited admission to
"any white male person." The courts decided that "the
affirmative declaration that male persons may be admitted is not an implied denial to the right of females."
Interestingly, a short time later the words "white male"
were dropped from the code. This too was on a
less-than-merit basis. A history of the Iowa University
College of Law tells us that, in order "to ridicule a
Republican amendment to strike out the word 'white' in
the bar admission bill, a Democrat suggested they might
as well strike out the word 'male' as well." So it was
done and women's history was made.

There was no flood of women to the bar, only the
slightest trickle—and still plenty of obstacles. At the
same time that Mrs. Mansfield was being admitted to
the bar, Mrs. Myra Bradwell was being turned down by
the State of Illinois, which said, in part, "That God
designed the sexes to occupy different spheres of action,
and that it belonged to men to make, apply, and execute

the laws was regarded as an almost axiomatic truth."
Miss Lemma Barkaloo became the first woman member
of the court to try a case in court. Later that year (1870)
Mrs. Ada H. Kepley graduated from the Union College
of Law in Chicago and became the first woman lawyer
to graduate from a law school in this country.

Slowly but surely universities and law schools opened
their doors, and states made provisions to admit women
to the bar. Shortly after the turn of the century the
National Association of Women Lawyers was formed
and female lawyers had their own organization and
their own platform. In its first issue, *The Women
Lawyers Journal* (May 1911) carried an article designed
to help female trial lawyers.

"Since the door has been opened in this country,
giving woman an opportunity to enter the field of the
law, in all those States where she is permitted to practice
she is accorded the same privileges as men. Not only
may she display her legal learning and sound professional judgment in the advice that she gives to the
clients whom she receives at her office, but she may
practice in all the courts of the States of which she is a
member of the bar, and, with the proper qualifications,
may distinguish herself in her work before judges and
juries.

"There are, however, some very definite requirements
which must be met before a woman can hope to make
her mark as a court lawyer.

"The principal drawbacks to a woman's success when
pitted against man in a legal battle are to be found in
the handicaps of sex. The voice, physical appearance,
and attire of the average woman lawyer do not produce

the impression of authority and aggressiveness which are characteristic of the average man lawyer. Legal ability alone cannot make up for lack of power and authority, and the woman who would succeed in jury trials should bear in mind the fact that one of the chief ways of impressing an audience is through the speaker's voice. A high-pitched, nervous-sounding voice carries little conviction with it, and the woman jury lawyer should, if necessary, prepare herself for her work by a special course of training in the art of effective speaking.

"In regard to her personal appearance, there are several things which the woman trial lawyer will do well to observe. She should never appear in court in anything but a dignified street costume, and it is advisable that she should remove her hat before addressing the judge. The tendency on the part of women to feel that their sex entitles them to receive, rather than to pay, deference should never be allowed to assert itself in the court room."

Today the legal profession, as it concerns female lawyers, is still operating as in those days of warning a lawyer "that she should remove her hat before addressing the judge." Though times are changing, relatively few women are judges in the United States and even fewer, a very elite few, sit on courts of wide jurisdiction. It would appear that women must continue to make their own gains. Male lawyers seem neither ready, willing, nor able to give female lawyers "a fair shake." Indeed, as we have noted, there has been and continues to be considerable opposition by men to female lawyers. One very eminent male lawyer reports:

"The emergence of women into fields formerly solely

dominated by men has not been met without opposition. In the law field, this is an example of one type of reaction. Northwestern University law professor Jack Coons, who readily admits that he is personally prejudiced against women lawyers, suggests that such qualms today stem largely from the fact that men's egos are more easily bruised. 'Their resentment of female competition,' he says, 'might be fear of the embarrassment of being beaten by a woman in a toe-to-toe struggle. Men are the weaker sex in terms of pride. In medicine, everyone wants the same result. In the law, someone has to lose whenever a case goes to judgment.' "

He then suggests a course of action for a woman interested in a career in law or in any other field: "She must learn to compete then, not as a woman, but as a human being. Not until a great many women move out of the fringes into the mainstream will society itself provide the arrangements for their new life plan. But every girl who manages to stick it out through law school or medical school, or who finishes her M.A. or Ph.D. and goes on to use it, helps others move on.

"Women are not men's equals; they have been subordinate to men for all of history. They will continue to be subordinate until they act as men's equals."

3
Time, Talent, and Tenacity

Dear Sir:

A young lady has applied to me for permission to become a student of law in my office. I advised her to seek admission into Yale Law School for one year and then enter my office. Are you far advanced enough to admit young women to your school? In theory I am in favor of their studying and practicing law provided they are *ugly,* but I should fear a handsome woman before a jury. Please let me know whether she could be admitted if she should desire to do so, also send me your circular or catalogue.

The letter was addressed to the Yale University Corporation on March 9, 1872, by George G. Sill, a graduate of Yale College. He was later to become lieutenant-governor of Connecticut.

Compare this with the pamphlet produced by Georgetown University "to encourage more women to pursue law as a profession:"

Law had long been one of society's most popular professions for ambitious college-educated men. There

Women students are still few and far between in most American law schools today, but the situation is slowly improving

is no good reason why law should not be as popular a
profession for women. The major deterrent to women is
the myth of women's proper role in society. It is not
easy to oppose society's traditional fantasies, such as:
"a woman can't mix a career with a family"; "intelligent
women are emasculating"; "women's decisions are
based on emotions, not logic." Although these attitudes
won't be easily changed, Georgetown University Law
Center realizes their invalidity and is committed to
encouraging you in your quest.

Getting into law school is not easy. There is still
plenty of discrimination against women by many old-
line schools. And, the discrimination starts before law
school, carries through it and picks up, unfortunately
with renewed vigor, after law school in the job market.
Despite all of this, according to the American Bar
Association (ABA) and the Association of American
Law Schools (AALS), two, three, and in some cases, five
times as many women are studying law today as were
only twenty years ago.

One noted law professor ascribes the influx of women
on law school campuses to "a number of reasons. In
general terms, I think the women's liberation movement
has heightened the consciousness of females in our
society to their worth and made contemporary undergraduate women more ready and willing to tackle
occupations traditionally thought of as men's work.
Until very recently, all but the brightest and hardest
driving women ruled themselves out of careers such as
the law because of the false impressions that they were
required to be superintellectuals and that they would
surely lose their femininity if they had to compete with
men in the courtroom."

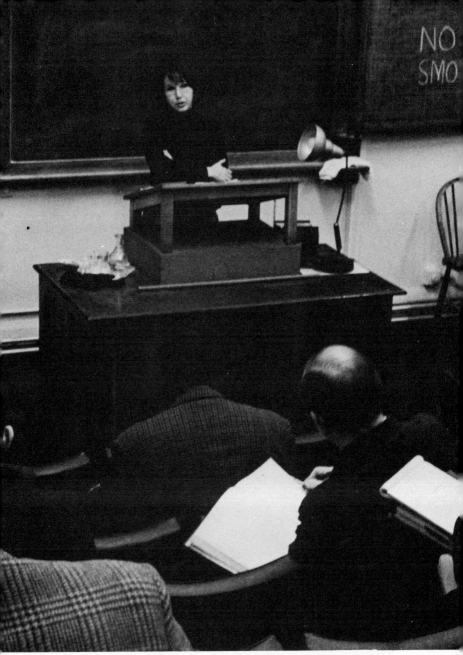

The lawyer speaks for the rights of man. Her broad background of skills must be built from high school days. Yet prejudice may still bar her from professorial positions, and Federal and local benches

A successful lawyer, a mother of two who practices law by herself adds, "Down through the years women have been their own worst enemies. They have to stop this self-selective process based on sex and just do their own thing, whatever it is."

What kind of profession is the law? What is it that lawyers do, day in and day out? We all know the stereotype of lawyer that has been passed to us by courtesy of radio, television, the movies, and the pages of books. He strides up and down in front of the jury making the most of every word, every gesture. His voice is first loud, then soft. Gentle, then harsh. Demanding, then pleading. He's never nervous and is always in command of the situation. He's Perry Mason or perhaps he's Superlawyer!

In everyday life a lawyer is considerably more than a high-powered courtroom performer. Our society demands that the lawyer fill many, many roles. To give prospective lawyers a peek into their future, the University of Pennsylvania projects its ideal composite lawyer:

> The lawyer is more than a skilled craftsman. She is concerned with the ends of law and the role of the lawyer in society.

> The lawyer speaks for the right of man. She has no higher duty than defense of individual liberty.

> The lawyer is a counselor. She advises people on varied and complex relationships with one another and the state. She advises government at all levels. In giving advice she brings into play her specialized understanding of the formal structure of society and of law as an instrument of social control and betterment.

She is an advocate. She represents the views, the needs, the aspirations, of others more effectively than they, uncounseled, are able to do by themselves.

She is an architect of social structure. She must respond to the need of a rapidly changing society for creativity and adaptiveness with respect to social structure and organization in both public and private sectors.

The lawyer is a social scientist. She draws upon history and experience for perspective in depth of human problems.

The lawyer is an educator, especially a self-educator. The process of educating a lawyer never ends. In every controversy she must refresh her expertise or acquire expertise in a new factual domain.

The lawyer is a leader. All her other qualifications converge in thrusting upon the lawyer leadership and responsibility in community life.

The lawyer is a planner, a negotiator, a peace-maker. Despite the popular stereotype of the lawyer as contentious adversary, the peaceful ordering of human relations overwhelmingly predominates in her activities. In the drafting of commercial and labor contracts, treaties, wills, constitutions, she is concerned with achieving orderly arrangements and with avoiding or settling controversy.

The lawyer is a humanist. To study law is to look through the greatest window on life. Here one sees the passions, the frailties, the aspirations, the baseness and the nobility of the human condition.

Because of all these roles and all that the public expects, the lawyer must acquire and use a wide range of knowledge, insight, and skill. The serious prospective lawyer starts this acquisition program while still in high school.

There are no specific courses to take, no specific areas to cover. A lawyer's education, starting in the middle years of high school, should be, says the AALS, "as broad as the universe of problems the lawyer faces." This general education should include everything necessary for acceptance by a liberal arts college or university and as much more as possible. This usually means 4 years of English; at least 2 years but preferably 3 years of mathematics; 3 years of social studies (including history, sociology, government, economics or political science); at least 2 years of science (including laboratory science); and at least 2 years but preferably more in either a modern or a classical foreign language. These "requirements" should be bolstered by any and all electives that offer experience or experimentation with writing, creative thinking, and understanding of the people and institutions in our modern world. Or, as the AALS comments, law "is a profession to which all of life is relevant. It deserves an education befitting its nature."

The foundation for success in law school and later on in a legal career is built at the undergraduate level. Students are advised to get as broad an education as possible, notes the Boston College Law School: "Because the field of law spans the entire social and commercial processes of our society, there is no collegiate program which cannot serve as an appropriate vehicle for prelegal training."

Few law schools specify particular courses or major

areas that must be taken by a prelaw student to qualify for admission. A typical answer to the question of prelaw studies comes from the Notre Dame Law School:

> The qualities which are most important for a law student to possess are not the product of any one course or combination of courses. They can be developed in any course which is well taught by an exacting teacher who requires his students to extend themselves. In the words of Chief Justice Stone, "The emphasis should be put on the intellectual discipline which the student derives from courses and [from] particular teachers, rather than [on] the selection of particular subjects without reference to the way in which they are taught."
>
> There are, though, two subjects which are recommended. A working knowledge of accounting is so helpful in the study of law that every pre-law student is urged to take some basic accounting. We find also that intensive work in English composition is especially useful in studying and practicing law. For the rest, college days should be devoted to the cultivation of intellectual and cultural interests and to the formation of habits of inquiry, of accuracy, and of intensive study. Any number of courses in various fields of learning will serve this purpose, if they are taught well by exacting teachers.

Where do you find the "right" college or university for your career? The right college for you? When you reach your junior year in high school you must add action to the process of thinking about a college education. Start early and you will have enough time to select rather than just settle. Procrastinate and you will be lucky to be able to settle for whatever you can get wherever you can get it.

Send for college catalogs during the fall and winter of your junior year so you can visit campuses and "take a look" at various schools during the more pleasant springtime months. As you try to decide on the right school, consider the following questions: Should it be a large school? A small one? Near home? Far away? Do you want a coeducational school? One that is church related? A well-known prestige school? What sort of academic level best suits you? What will your schooling cost? Can you expect some financial assistance from home or scholarship money from the school?

Because it is virtually impossible to survey all the colleges and universities, the wise high school student lets someone else do the research. There are several excellent books that will give you the information required and allow you to make an intelligent decision. Our favorite is *The New York Times Guide to College Selection.*

When you arrive at college be prepared to learn, to think, to experiment, to enjoy. A college education is not all "nose to the grindstone." There must be some play to go along with all the work. Simply stated, you must be determined to get the best and broadest education possible using required courses (for your major and degree) as the solid foundation on which to build all the related and frequently unrelated courses you want to take. This does not give you room to take snap or cinch courses. It also does not allow or include the so-called law courses that are given on the under-graduate level. These courses, says the AALS, are

The prospective law student should visit campuses and gather impressions. Scenes like this featuring women law students are still rare

"generally not intended as education for lawyers but for other purposes."

Because there is no specific list of courses that law schools require to be completed so that a student may be eligible for admission, it is sometimes difficult to know whether you are getting enough of one subject or too little of another. The AALS states: "What the law schools seek in their entering students is not accomplishment in mere memorization but accomplishment in understanding, the capacity to think for themselves, and the ability to express their thoughts with clarity and force."

The University of Illinois College of Law offers some suggestions for guidance in choosing undergraduate courses for students interested in law careers, categorized as:

(1) Ability to comprehend others and express oneself.
(2) Ability to think creatively and critically.
(3) Ability to understand human institutions and values with which the law deals.

The university then suggests that the abilities you need are as basic to you as the three R's were to your grandparents. At first glance they may appear to be extremely simple accomplishments—ones you probably feel are not to be mentioned in the same breath with so sophisticated a profession as the law. Take a closer look and you will see that they are skills which can be developed to different levels, and your ability first as a law student and later as a lawyer will depend greatly on how far you develop each of them.

If a lawyer is to be effective, she must be precise in

the use of language—both spoken and written. By speaking, we mean more than just being able to carry on a conversation or to express your desires; more is meant than oratory, a pleasant voice, or the incitement of an emotional response in your listener. You must develop the ability to communicate—to convey and drive home the ideas and thoughts contained in your mind to the mind of another. The old idea of the lawyer as a bombastic trial orator is out-of-date, but the contemporary lawyer probably talks professionally even more today than ever before. She must speak to judges, juries, clients, associates, revenue agents, boards of directors, witnesses, and fellow lawyers. Often the modern lawyer is dealing with the small but select audience of the conference table. To whomever the lawyer is communicating, she must impart an exact and complete impression of her meaning.

The lawyer is required to do a great deal of writing. A brief, a will, a contract, a trust agreement, an opinion— all are among the everyday tasks of the lawyer. In writing, as well as in speaking, she must be able to use language that carries her meaning to others accurately, concisely, and forcefully. For example, when the maker of a will dies, the will carries the final expression of his wishes for the disposition of his property. Obviously, after death the maker is not available to clarify or explain cloudy or inaccurate expressions. The courts and others may be required to interpret the language of the will to determine how the maker's property should be distributed. The lawyer who wrote the will inaccurately cannot then say to the court, "I should have said it this way," since the language of the will alone is authoritative.

By now you should be able to see that "language is the lawyer's working tool," and a person who wishes to be a lawyer must be well trained in the art of verbal expression. This means that the undergraduate student must develop an adequate vocabulary, proficiency in modern English usage, grammatical correctness, conciseness, clarity of statement, and skill in organizing a presentation whether oral or written. The student must also become sensitive to shades of meaning, problems of ambiguity, the variable meaning of words depending on context, use of emotionally charged words, catch phrases, and empty generalizations.

Comprehension includes the capacity to understand what is read and heard. It is not enough that the printed page be read or that the spoken word be heard; the meaning of the author or speaker must be accurately understood. The lawyer must quickly and firmly get the exact meaning of oral statements and legal instruments, catch the fine points of legal reasoning and argument, assimilate the technical materials that constitute the body of the law, and understand the often inaccurate and imprecise conversation or writing of others. She must not be naïve and accept words that sound important but are, in fact, either false or irrelevant. In both reading and listening comprehension, the lawyer must detect and select fact from opinion, the relevant from the irrelevant, the important from the unimportant. The following undergraduate courses are highly recommended as a means of developing the skills of comprehension and expression: English grammar and composition or rhetoric, English literature, public speaking, and advanced courses in the humanities and

Women Law Students, Duke University

Preparation for law school involves disciplines rather than special subjects. Here law students meet between lectures and chat or check posted grades listed by number codes

the social sciences that require extensive reading and writing. In addition to formal course studies you should continually increase your capacity for expression and understanding by reading widely and participating in extracurricular activities involving writing, speaking, and debating.

Whether the lawyer is general practitioner, administrator, judge, legislator, or scholar, much of her work will call for problem-solving and sound judgment. This requires skill in thinking both critically and creatively. As a lawyer you must recognize and comprehend the significance of facts, organize them, examine them in the light of established legal principles, and make predictions with respect to them so that you can advise a client on the manner in which he can conduct himself with a maximum of freedom from legal difficulty. To make a prediction you must be able to examine the facts and the applicable rules of law with a critical attitude. To help a client you will often have to create specially tailored legal solutions to his problems.

Be certain to cultivate your ability to think critically while in college. Try to be skeptical and completely curious. Develop a thoroughness of inquiry and the ability to cut through to essentials. Also be able to avoid preconceptions, be willing to recognize all facts, and be capable of withholding judgment until all facts are considered. In short, critical thinking means being thorough and being intellectually honest with yourself in appraising any situation.

The lawyer's opportunity to exercise creative thinking will come from an almost never ending number of legal relationships. Anything you do as a lawyer can be done better if you are capable of creative thinking. You may be preparing a simple contract between a buyer and a seller of goods, or you may be tailoring a very complex corporate structure for the specific needs of a business or a nonprofit organization. You may be designing legislation to deal with a social problem, or you may be deciding a difficult case involving a precedent of consequence. To do any of these you must develop skill in organizing factual materials, formulating principles from raw data, reasoning by analogy, making decisions in the light of short- and long-term goals, and being able to use broad theoretical knowledge in specific situations.

It is doubtful that you will find a course in thinking—creative, critical, or otherwise—in any college catalog. You will, however, find courses in logic, which can give you insight into the theory of rational thinking. You will also find courses that describe and categorize methods of reasoning and types of arguments. Courses in philosophy offer you the opportunity to observe in action both the critical and the creative thought of some of the world's great thinkers. Mathematics and advanced courses in the physical sciences offer excellent training in reasoning with abstractions, although the expression of such abstractions will be made in precise mathematical formulas. Law involves reasoning in abstractions, but these are not expressed in precise terms. As a result, it is important that your skill in comprehension and expression be developed to the point that you can reason with abstract concepts that cannot always be stated precisely. The study of a laboratory science will provide you with valuable experience in thorough observation and critical evaluation of facts as well as the use of inductive reasoning from particular facts that you can see to a general conclusion. In law you will often be required to reason in a similar fashion from particular decided cases to general rules and principles.

The rules of law as set forth in statutes, reported judicial decisions, and legal texts are the hard-core foundation of your legal education. But they are not a self-contained system independent of the day-to-day activity of the human race. The contrary is closer to the truth. Law is an evolutionary institution. It is always being changed by a changing society, and it, in turn, changes society.

Your professional knowledge as a lawyer must amount to more than an expertise in legal rules and legal craftsmanship. It must include an understanding of the way human institutions and values affect the operation of the law and the way the law affects society. As a matter of daily professional work, the lawyer-legislator, the lawyer-judge, the lawyer-administrator, and the lawyer-board member must decide matters of policy requiring a very broad knowledge of social values even though their duties fall within the framework of legal rules. The private practitioner deals daily with such human institutions as business and competition, marriage and the family, government and the taxpayer, private property and its use, and the regulations of human activity by numerous boards, agencies, legislatures, courts, bureaus, and councils. She can do her work competently only if she knows how and why these people function. She also has a professional obligation to constantly improve the laws and know how these laws are carried out within the part of the world she sees every day. To improve legal rules requires more than a knowledge of those rules.

As a result, the lawyer, because of her expert knowledge of the rules by which society is guided, is normally thrust into positions of social leadership with responsibilities that require a very broad education. Of all professional people, the lawyer must have the widest range of knowledge.

As you can see, it is important that your undergraduate training include the development of a broad insight into human nature and society and a cultivation of historical consciousness. It is impossible, of course, to study every relevant academic subject in detail, and we therefore suggest intensive concentration in one or two of the following general subject areas: (1) the economic area—economic systems, business practices, theories of business and the economy, the role of government in the economy; (2) the governmental area—political organizations, basic political theories, the democratic process, the role of education, the moral considerations involved in the art of government; (3) the human area—individual personality, social mores and customs, man's abilities and limitations in learning and planning conduct, the functions of groups such as the family and the church, the problems of a typical person, social control by governmental means; and (4) the heritage of Western society—Greek, Roman, and Christian traditions and ideas; the evolution of the concept of individual freedom; the art of peaceful, orderly adaptation to change; historical theories of the relationship between the individual and the state.

From this you can see that a major field of study could very profitably be chosen from any of the following academic subjects: economics, political science, philosophy (including ethics), psychology, sociology, anthropology, literature, and history. The choice of any one of these subjects will also tie in well with the development of your skill in thinking, comprehension, and expression.

Rounding out the suggestions for undergraduate study, the AALS adds:

"Accounting is a practical study of which lawyers must have some appreciation, as it is in many respects the very language of business. The student would be wise to learn it in college, but, if he has not, he will probably want to master at least its rudiments in law school.

"Lawyers have adapted more slowly than many to the new technologies of information retrieval, communication, and document preparation. You can do very well in law school with no knowledge of computers, but they will affect legal work and research increasingly in the future. The law student who has some understanding of them will be better equipped for work in the 1980's and beyond."

With all these courses safely under your belt, you should now be ready to go about the business of getting into a law school.

Skills in thinking, comprehension, and expression win admittance to law school and even a spot on the law review, a high honor and springboard for later employment

4
Onward and Upward to Law School

"To an increasing number of college graduates, law offers the possibility of reforming society from 'within the system' while at the same time providing a rich variety of job opportunities. As a result, there are virtually no empty places in the nation's law schools. Huge numbers of applicants are being denied admission by schools they would not have deigned to consider only a few years ago."

This report by *The New York Times* in January 1973 bears out an ABA survey that found "there were no spaces whatever at all but three of the law schools." Not very encouraging, but does it mean that you had better find a different career?

Not at all. It simply means you must set your academic goals higher and work even harder than you had planned, so that you will be "among the chosen few." You must also be able to present yourself as the kind of student and person who would make a good lawyer. With seats in law schools as scarce as they are and no prospect of more available in the immediate future, law schools are understandably unhappy about even a single "wasted" admission.

Perhaps the first time you "plead a case" it will be for yourself, and you won't even be there in person. This will take place as your application and supporting materials are reviewed by an admissions committee, the dean of a particular law school, the director of admissions, or any combination of these. In their minds will be the number of first-year seats available and the desire to fill them with "the cream of the crop." In their hands will be your file, which typically contains your college transcript, the score of your Law School Admission Test (LSAT), your application form and residency documents where required, indication that an application fee has been paid, recommendations where requested, and whatever other documents are relevant to your application.

Many prospective lawyers are convinced that the combination of grade-point average (GPA) based on their undergraduate work and LSAT score are the be-all and end-all of law school admission. This is not entirely true, but it would be foolish to minimize their importance to the admissions decision-making process. The AALS suggests that the GPA/LSAT score combination is the most important factor considered for admission to a law school. However, the organization is also quick to suggest: "Reliance on these two numerical predictors as a generally proven starting point has led to the mistaken impression among many applicants that admissions decision-making is a purely numerical process.

"The examination and consideration of nonnumerical factors are an important part of the decision-making process in all cases, and especially so in cases where the decision is a close one. They account for much of the time spent by admissions committees. There may be indications that the numerical factors are unreliable in a particular case, or are outweighed by other factors. It may be important that the applicant is a state resident or comes from far away, that he is a member of a minority group that ought to be better represented in law school and the profession, or that he has an interesting background of nonacademic experience. The law schools will consider such factors as the caliber of the applicant's college, extracurricular activities, the trend of his grades, letters of recommendation, work experience during and after college, graduate studies, service in the military, Peace Corps, VISTA, and the like, and the applicant's statement about himself and his purposes."

Now that you know that all kinds of people are accepted into law schools—not only the brilliant, the rich, and the well known—the actual application procedure should take on added importance for you. Here, once again, you have some decision-making to do. You must decide, on the basis of your credentials and some careful research, which is the "right" law school for you. You can use the "shotgun" approach favored by many students: the lower their GPA/LSAT score combination, the more applications they send out. A far better and considerably more "scientific" approach is to match your credentials with those listed by various law schools. After completing your survey, you can apply to those schools whose admission standards give you a reasonable chance for success. You can find grade-point

Admission into law school depends on many factors besides the academic one. Once the admissions hurdle is crossed, a school like the University of Notre Dame allows women to participate on an equal basis with men—even in sports and extracurricular activities

averages and LSAT requirements for most accredited law schools in the *Prelaw Handbook*, available for a nominal amount from Law School Admission Council, Educational Testing Service, Box 944, Princeton, N.J. 08540.

Armed with the knowledge that you at least stand a chance for admission to several law schools, use some of the following criteria to select the "highest quality" law school in your grouping.

First, find out about the faculty by checking law school catalogs. Just about all of them list the educational achievements of the faculty, so you can easily make up a box score. The school whose faculty has the most advanced degrees (past the J.D. or LL.B., which must be considered basic) should be considered the most desirable.

While you are researching faculty members, check their rank and their nonteaching experience. The most desirable school is the one with the largest number of full professors in each of the study areas. Schools whose teaching ranks are fat with assistant and associate professors and lecturers and instructors and very thin in full professors are not nearly so desirable. Similarly, the school with the greatest number of faculty members who have years of excellent experience in particular fields is far more attractive than the school staffed with law school graduates who have never tasted victory or defeat in actual cases and situations.

Another measuring stick you can use to pick the "right" law school is the law library. The number of books in the law school library and the rate at which new volumes are acquired will give you an idea of the

Because so much law work entails research, the size and currency of
the library is an important measuring stick in selecting a law school

school with the most comprehensive collection. All other things being equal, the school with the largest library should be the one you select.

There are several other factors you can check and should consider as you prepare to apply to law schools. For example: What is the student-faculty ratio? About 20:1 is average. How large are first-year classes? The larger they are the less attention you'll get. What is the freshman attrition rate? Usually, the higher the rate, the lower the admission standards. What is offered in the curriculum? Most are similar, but differences can show faculty strengths and weaknesses.

Applying for admission to law schools is simple if directions are followed and careful attention is paid to details. There are several parts to each application file, and it is your job to be certain that all the pieces fall into position at the right place and time. The first step is to send postcards requesting catalogs and application materials from the schools you have selected. This should be done in the fall of the year preceding enrollment.

At the same time make arrangements to take the LSAT and register for the Law School Data Assembly Service (LSDAS), but more about these later. When your application forms arrive, read them carefully, fill them out *exactly* as instructed, and return them as quickly as possible to the law school. Some schools act on applications as they are received (rolling admissions), while others wait until after a certain date and then act on them in the order in which they were filed. In either case it is to your advantage to get your application in as quickly as possible. And it must be complete. Send everything requested. Admissions officers act only on complete files and reject all incomplete ones.

Though promptness is important, accuracy, attention to detail, and clarity in writing are even more important. Don't take the chance of losing out on a fine law school because of a poor impression made by your application. Be complete without being wordy. Be accurate without irrelevant details. Be careful without being stilted.

Many application forms give you the opportunity to write a short essay or at least a few paragraphs in an open-ended question. Use this to your best advantage. Show yourself off. Say what you think. Above all, be honest. Don't write the kind of stuff you think the admissions committee will like—write the kind of stuff you believe.

To give you an idea of these open-ended questions, here are a few samples:

"On a separate sheet, in 200 to 500 words state your reasons for studying law."

"Indicate in the space below your reasons for desiring to study law, and the reasons why you believe you are qualified for the study or practice of law. Unusual factors which you believe the Committee should know about you should be outlined in this section. Confine your remarks to the space below, or no more than one additional page. Do not submit additional materials (e.g., term papers, etc.)."

"The Admissions Committee believes that all relevant factors should be considered when selecting an entering class. The space below provides an opportunity for all applicants to present themselves and their qualifications as they wish. Applicants may wish to explain or to draw the attention of the Committee to a particular part of their record or application. They may also wish the Committee to consider achievements and qualities not otherwise revealed by the application. Additionally, this form may be used to complete answers to questions on the application or to make any other comments which the applicant believes are relevant."

Getting back to the LSAT: The Educational Testing Service, administrator of the exam, describes it as:

"A half-day objective test, given five times a year, designed to measure certain mental capacities important in the study of law: general academic ability at a suitable level and command of written English. It yields an LSAT score and a writing ability score. The LSAT portion measures your ability to understand and reason with a variety of verbal, quantitative, and symbolic materials. The writing ability portion measures your facility in using standard English to express ideas clearly, precisely, and forcefully. Both portions thus assess your intellectual skills, not your grasp of specific subjects.

"Submission of an LSAT score is an admission requirement at most American law schools." (See Appendix listing for each law school.)

To help students familiarize themselves with the test and procedures, and to provide an application form, a booklet called *Law School Admission Bulletin* can be obtained from Educational Testing Service, Box 944, Princeton, N.J. 08540.

A few important points to remember about the LSAT:

1. Application for the test is *only* application for the test. It is not an application to a law school. Application to law schools must be made separately.

2. The exam should be taken at least eight weeks prior to the law school's application deadline. This will allow your scores to be included with your file in time to be considered by the admissions committee.

3. Don't worry about the exam and don't study or cram for it. Familiarize yourself with the mechanics of the exam by reading the *Bulletin* and doing the sample questions. Says the ETS, "Since the LSAT measures intellectual qualities that develop gradually and types of knowledge that one accumulates over relatively long periods of time, no specific preparation can be made immediately before the test. There is no evidence that taking cram courses or studying review books results in significant score gains."

4. If your college participates in the LSDAS, register for it at the same time you register for the LSAT. (See Appendix listing for each law school.) The ETS describes this service by saying that it "collects transcripts of your academic work (undergraduate, graduate, and professional, including law school, if any); summarizes your undergraduate transcripts into a uniform format; and sends an LSDAS report, containing your LSAT score, the summaries of your undergraduate transcripts, and information from your Registration Form, plus a copy of each transcript to each law school you designate. You will receive a shortened version of the report.

"Registration for LSDAS is valid only for the current processing year, but you need register only once regardless of how often you wish to use the service during that year.

"The LSDAS reports are intended to simplify and reduce the clerical work in law school admissions offices. The reports are not substitutes for college transcripts nor the reasoned judgment of admissions officers. The LSDAS reports make no judgment about the quality of your credentials nor about your chances of being admitted to law school."

Still another service, the Graduate and Professional School Financial Aid Service (GAPSFAS), can help with the very practical problem of financing your law school education. If finances are not a problem, or at best a minor one, congratulations. If finances are a major problem, look into GAPSFAS which "simplifies financial aid procedures and the collection of information from applicants, their spouses (or spouses-to-be), and their parents.

"If you want to apply for aid from participating law schools (check the law school's catalog for participation information), you must submit to the GAPSFAS information concerning your own and your spouse's (or spouse-to-be) financial resources and obligations as well as a statement regarding your parents' resources; this requirement applies even though you may consider yourself self-supporting. The GAPSFAS will send a copy of the questionnaires on you and your spouse (or spouse-to-be) plus an analysis of your own, your spouse's (or spouse-to-be), and your parents' financial resources to each law school you designate.

"If you are interested in obtaining financial assistance from other kinds of professional or graduate schools, you may use your GAPSFAS form to apply to them also. You must however, submit information concerning your spouse (or spouse-to-be) and parents to qualify for aid at law schools even if some graduate or professional schools to which you may apply do not require it.

"Since most law schools make financial aid decisions soon after an applicant is admitted, submit your GAPSFAS form at the same time—or soon after—you send your other application papers, if possible. A law school that uses this financial aid service will take no action on a request for financial aid until it has received your analyzed GAPSFAS application."

O.K., all of this has been completed, you've been waiting and praying for several weeks, and then finally the word comes . . . you've been accepted for law school and are to start in the fall. What can you expect?

Perhaps the best way to answer that question is to look at the aims and purposes statement of a well-known law school:

The program of study—including the curriculum, the teaching methods, and extracurricular activities—is designed to prepare the student for participation in the varied activities of the profession of law and to lay the basis for professional competence in any jurisdiction where the Anglo-American system of jurisprudence prevails. Emphasis is placed on the development of the legal skills of analysis, organization, fact discrimination and presentation, argumentation, draftsmanship and legal planning, counseling, and negotiation. Essential to proficiency in legal reasoning and competence in legal methods is an awareness by the student that law is not merely a series of rules, but a process of adjusting human relationships in an organized society.

The Law School seeks to create this awareness by giving the student an understanding of the legal system as a working whole and an appreciation of law in its relationship to other agencies of social control and other disciplines of learning. Throughout his law school course the student is not only expected to become familiar with the significant legal rules, standards, and principles but also to assess their social, economic, and political implications and to determine their relevance to existing community problems. Law is the accepted means of providing necessary social controls as needs are created or revealed by developments in other fields. The student learns that solutions to complicated problems are found by joining legal knowledge and ingenuity with knowledge of the physical and social sciences.

The school seeks to instill in the student a feeling of the dignity, responsibilities, and traditions of the legal profession. To this end, it makes a special effort to create in him an awareness of (*a*) the lawyer's responsibility to keep acquainted fully with significant developments in his community, in business, and in government at all levels; (*b*) the lawyer's role as moulder of public opinion; and (*c*) the lawyer's obligation to provide civic leadership.

The usual, though not exclusive, method of instruction is the case method. This method, in which the instructor and student engage in a free discussion of selected cases, requires a careful analysis of individual cases and a synthesis of groups of cases, to draw out the principles of the common law according to the method by which they were developed. To be most effective, the case method has three requirements: a skilled and able instructor, thoroughly expert in his subject, who delights in the teaching process; a comparatively small class;

To give experience in trial technique, a practice or "moot court" gives students a chance at playing each courtroom role, except judge—the professor's province. Here women play jurors, though in some states women may not be called for jury duty

and an alert and properly conditioned group of students, with each member participating actively in the discussion. Given these factors, a law class can become an intensely stimulating process involving a high degree of intellectual enjoyment. The School of Law has striven consciously and successfully to meet these three requirements in a preeminent fashion. Variations from this method—e.g., counseling and planning problems, drafting exercises, experiences in trial technique, memorandum and brief writing, and appellate argument—are used to round out the skills of the lawyer's craft.

Another fine school adds:

The first-term curriculum for candidates matriculating for the degree of J.D. is prescribed. It is an attempt to introduce the core of Anglo-American legal reasoning and legal culture through four courses: Constitutional Law, Contracts, Procedure, and Torts. One of these courses is taught in a small group, normally not more than twenty students, in which the student is tutored in legal research and writing. For the remaining five terms, a student is free to select his own curriculum, the only remaining course requirements being Criminal Law, enrollment in a forensic or legal-service program, and supervised analytic writing in six units of courses, seminars, or special programs.

Knowing that there are few, if any, required courses after the first year doesn't make the task presented by law school any less awesome. Indeed, a look at the following typical program from a "good" law school will show the universality of the legal profession and of a law school education.

First-Year Courses

Fall	Hours	Spring	Hours
Contracts	3	Constitutional Law*	3
Criminal Justice	3	Contracts	2
Introduction to		Criminal Procedure*	3
Property	3	Practice Training II	2
Practice Training I	1	Private Land-Use Controls	3
Procedure I	3	Procedure I	3
Tort Law and		Tort Law and Alternatives	2
Alternatives	3		

*Elect one

Second-Year Electives

Fall	Hours	Spring	Hours
Basic Commercial Law	3	Business Enterprises II	3
Business Enterprises I	3	Commercial Paper and	
Trusts and Estates I	3	Banking Transactions	2
		Legal Accounting	2
		Trusts and Estates II	3

Third-Year Electives

Fall	Hours	Spring	Hours
Conflict of Laws	3	Comparative State Proce-	
Evidence	3	dure	3
Federal Jurisdiction	2	Creditors' Rights and	
Procedure II	3	Secured Transactions	3
		Procedure II	3

SECOND- OR THIRD-YEAR ELECTIVES

Fall	Hours	Spring	Hours
Admiralty	2	Administrative Law	3
Domestic Relations	2	Antitrust and Trade	
Estate and Gift Tax	2	Regulation	3
Environmental Law	2	Comparative Law	3
International Law	3	Criminal Procedure	3
Labor Law I	3	Housing and Urban	
Land Financing	3	Development	2
Remedies	3	Income Taxation	3
Welfare Law	3	Insurance	2
		Labor Law II	2
		Land-Use Planning	3
		Legal Philosophy	2
		Local Government	3
		Securities Regulation	3
		Taxation of Business	
		Enterprises	3

PROBLEM COURSES

Fall	Hours	Spring	Hours
Corporate Practice	2	Civil Rights	2
Estate Planning	2	Copyright, Trademark,	
Government Contracts	2	and Patent Law	2
Legal Interviewing and		Fiduciary Administration	2
Counseling	2	International Business	
Legislation	2	Transactions	2
Litigation of Business		Law Practice Dynamics	2
Disputes—Domestic		Prisoner Representation	2
and International	2	Problems of Urban	
Prisoner Representation	2	Development	2
Problems of Clinical Law	2	Science, Technology,	
Trial and Appellate		and Law	2
Advocacy	2		

As you can see, law school is exciting, it is dynamic, and it is as modern and up-to-date as tomorrow. Each day brings changes that you as a lawyer must know, understand, and be ready to use. While there is an overabundance of work and study in law school, the rewards are great, in both personal and practical satisfaction.

It is said that the best students, those on law review or in the top 10 percent of their class, have marvelous career opportunities waiting for them. The others, the average and the little bit better-than-average students, have a tougher row to hoe in getting started and gaining the kind of career send-off we all envision. Law school is one of the places in our world that has a direct payoff into the future which is tied to good grades. Obviously, in most cases, the payoff is well worth the effort you must expend to qualify for it.

A word about exams and admission to the bar. All states require bar exams in one form or another. With your law school diploma in hand, you still have the hurdle of the bar exam if you want to practice as a full-fledged lawyer. The same is true if you have been practicing in one state and wish to practice in another. Once again it is back to school, this time for a six-to-ten-week cram course to prepare you for the bar exam in the jurisdiction in which you wish to practice.

In addition, many states require law students to register with the State Board of Law Examiners before entering law school. Some states have special requirements concerning prelegal training, domicile, appointment of a preceptor, certificates of character and fitness, and the study of "professional ethics." Be sure you check the rules of the state in which you expect to practice before you start law school so you can be certain that you will meet all the requirements. Remember, you are governed by the rules of the state in which you will practice, not the state in which you received your diploma from law school.

With all this schooling, studying, and testing behind you, you are now ready to start really learning in the toughest school of them all—the school of everyday life.

5

Specialties
Are the Case

"And there's the guy who smiled and said he hoped I wasn't like the one woman who had worked for his firm: she had been determined to work *only* in fields like labor law, where no women worked. What I don't understand is why that was considered so awful, and yet offering me jobs *only* in fields where women worked was considered acceptable and reasonable. Neither concept makes any sense to me," is the way a female Harvard Law School graduate typified her job interviews. So long as she remained within the area of "women's subjects" she could get a job. When she tried to get into the traditionally "masculine" areas, she was told she couldn't because clients wouldn't like working with women lawyers.

Making the situation even more ludicrous than it actually is, the ABA "does not formally recognize any specialization within law practice except that of patent law." However, the president of the Association has said, "At least some degree of specialization is obviously an existing necessity of modern law practice, and it properly should be. The complexity of our society and the increasing participation therein by government make it clear that no individual lawyer can be proficient in the performance of all legal tasks. I believe that our ever-expanding economy will inevitably lead to an ever-increasing pattern of specialization by practicing lawyers in a limited number of the various fields of law practice. State bars and their pilot programs will provide the answers the ABA is seeking in this important challenge to the obsolete myth that a lawyer can be a jack of all legal trades."

Though, as we can see, legal specialization has not as yet been legitimatized, it is being practiced, nonetheless, either deliberately or because "that's the way the ball bounces." Few lawyers actually specialize while in law school. Similarly a doctor does not specialize while still in medical school. However, the difference is that a doctor is expected to go on to specialize during her residency, which is still a part of her formal training. For the lawyer, specialization usually comes after she begins practicing because: (1) the cases she gets all seem to be in the same legal area and the more she gets, the better her reputation becomes, (2) she's working in a large law firm and they need someone in a specific area, (3) she's working with an experienced lawyer and she/he teaches her the "tricks of the trade" in a specialized area, (4) she likes one kind of law and goes out of her way to become proficient in it, including going to graduate school.

Whatever the method used to specialize, it is a good idea to know a bit about some of the legal "specialties" so you can orient your thinking either toward or away from any of them.

ADMINISTRATIVE LAW is concerned with the processes of lawmaking and their application by the government's executive departments and their control by the legislative and judicial departments. Of special interest to administrative lawyers are the "independent" regulatory agencies and the "tension between law and discretion, between the need for grants of power sufficient to ensure effective government and the need to limit that power to protect the citizen from government oppression or unfairness." Some of the areas that fall within the administrative lawyer's interest today are the regulation of natural monopolies, rent control, the allocation of radio and television frequencies, the design of railroad rates, labor regulation, Securities and Exchange Commission (SEC) and Federal Trade Commission (FTC) disclosure, and the requirement of truth in advertising. It focuses on contemporary issues, including the right to notice and the opportunity to be heard, adequacy of notice, right of representation by counsel, constitution of a fair hearing, and other aspects that maintain and support our tradition of liberty under the law.

ADMIRALTY LAW is sometimes called maritime law and is concerned with commerce and navigation on the high seas as well as on any navigable waters, including rivers and inland lakes. Maritime law is frequently very different from land law and from the laws that govern other modes of transportation. Though there are general maritime laws that apply all over the world, they are administered and interpreted in each country according to the laws, customs, and courts of that country. Some of the areas covered by admiralty law include contracts, insurance, personal injury, damage, collision, salvage, property, and any acts that break laws at sea or pertaining to the sea. Admiralty lawyers usually practice in the largest seaport cities here and abroad.

CORPORATION LAW is concerned with the legal rights, responsibilities, and privileges of large corporations in their dealings with government and with their customers. Corporation lawyers advise their clients on all laws, statutes, and decisions as they affect or may affect the corporations. They are also involved in policy decisions of large corporations concerning stocks and bonds, rights of stockholders, powers of boards of directors, and other legal-based matters. Corporation lawyers may be called upon to negotiate contracts or other transactions on behalf of their clients, represent them in labor negotiations, and prosecute in or defend them against a lawsuit. The corporation lawyer may also be asked to advise clients on such matters as corporate organization and reorganization, taxation, antitrust and trade regulations, and licensing. These corporate law specialists may be in private practice, they may be the "experts" in a large law firm, they may be in the legal department of a specific corporation, or they may be employed by the Federal Government. The field grows and grows, keeping pace with the increased interaction between government and business on many, many levels.

Two criminal lawyers "behind bars" to explain their rights to prisoners who may be able to leave their jail cells once bail has been arranged

CRIMINAL LAW is probably the best publicized and most glamorous specialty in the legal profession. Yet many lawyers shun it as distasteful, others because it is less profitable than some areas, and still others for both reasons. Some dedicated attorneys find this area of the law specially rewarding and perform very important public services as a public defender to represent defendants who cannot afford private counsel. In the course of regular practice the criminal lawyer comes in contact with all kinds of people, both innocent and guilty. She concentrates on all the crimes against society—murder, rape, theft, arson. She takes the case from the very beginning to its natural conclusion, be that freedom for a client or jail after allowable appeals. The criminal lawyer investigates the case; interviews clients and witnesses; researches the particular law and situation; examines, cross-examines, and conducts the trial in the courtroom; and then pleads the case to the jury. This area of law is not for the fainthearted. However, for those who follow it there are considerable rewards.

FAMILY LAW is the specialty involved with all aspects of legal problems of family life. It includes the problems and remedies of family relationships that come into being after the marriage ceremony or in a common-law marriage or as a result of children born out of wedlock. It is concerned with the legal relationships between husband and wife and between parent and child, including the adoption of children and responsibilities in juvenile court matters. It also covers the breakup of a family as the result of annulment, separation, and divorce, with such matters as grounds and defenses,

jurisdiction, alimony, custody of children, and agreements between disputants. Because these specialists are
dealing with families and with children, it is especially
important that every avenue to compromise, counseling,
and agreement be reached between the parties so that
litigation may be avoided. Many feel it is in this area
that lawyers have "their finest hours."

INTERNATIONAL AND COMPARATIVE LAW is
concerned with the basic contemporary problems involving the law and its effectiveness throughout the
world as one nation deals with another. In addition to
the obvious matters of treaties, rights of civilians, and
international contracts, this very specialized field of law
is vitally concerned with international organizations;
control of the use of force in international affairs;
control of the use of sea, air, and space; peaceful
settlement of international disputes; recognition of
states and governments; governmental immunities; and
jurisdiction of states over persons and territories.

The comparative law portion of this specialty is
particularly interested in understanding and using the
fundamental differences and the common features of
the various legal systems existing throughout the world.
Lawyers trained in these areas are able to practice in
American as well as foreign courts because they are
conversant with the French, German, and Swiss law
models—the recognized outstanding codes. Naturally, a
great many international and comparative lawyers work
for the U.S. Government's Department of State and
other diplomatic and consular governmental organizations.

LABOR LAW comes into the public eye when there is a strike or the threat of a strike in a vital industry or company. Fortunately this kind of cliff-hanging situation doesn't happen too often—usually because of the behind-the-scenes efforts of experienced labor lawyers. With the history of labor law as their guide, these specialists are prepared to negotiate between labor and management; set up collective-bargaining agreements; advise on such matters as wages, hours, and employee working conditions; and act as arbitrators in major disputes. Labor lawyers are also called upon to represent their clients before the courts in labor matters and before such groups as the National Labor Relations Board to settle union jurisdictional matters and claims of unfair labor practices. Representing employee groups or unions, the labor lawyer is concerned with such matters as discrimination, rights of employees, fair representation, unemployment compensation insurance, wages and hours, and pension rights.

PATENT, TRADEMARK, AND COPYRIGHT LAW touches every area of life where products are made, materials are read, and actions are watched. The reason for this is the clause in our Constitution empowering Congress "to promote the progress of science and useful arts, by securing for limited times to authors and inventors the exclusive right to their respective writings and discoveries." Patent lawyers advise clients on the classes of patentable materials; their rights within the patent law; the prerequisites of novelty, utility, and nonobviousness required to obtain a patent; infringement of rights; licensing; and patent misuse. Lawyers

Coping with intricate contracts can be confusing for the layman. Here attorneys explain "the fine print" to their client as she prepares to sign a document

practicing in the field of patent law obtain patents after a thorough search has been made and an exact description of the item drawn up. Frequently patent lawyers are also copyright experts and can work with artists, entertainers, and writers to protect their works and talents from plagiarism and other illegal use. Some of the types of works that come under copyright protection are books, periodicals, maps, musical works, photographic works, movies, television programs, commercial prints and labels, and artistic designs. Trademark law protects the mark and good name of a company against persons who try to use or copy a mark that is easily recognizable and has considerable value.

TAXATION LAW cuts across a great many legal areas affecting each of us in our private and business lives. Tax law specialists advise their clients on such matters as income and business taxes, and represent them when questions arise before the Internal Revenue Service or in the courts. Because of the degree of specialization in this area, other lawyers frequently call on tax lawyers for additional client counseling. Some of the subjects that fall within the tax lawyer's expertise are federal income taxation, corporate income taxation, foreign taxation, estate planning, deferred compensation, federal estate and gift taxation, income taxation of partners and partnerships, state and local taxation, tax-exempt organization, tax penalties and prosecutions, U.S. taxation of foreign income and aliens. As this field continues to grow because of increased activity in tax legislation on every level, opportunities for successful careers also continue to grow.

These are but a very few of the specialized areas of practice in the legal profession. Some other areas of law worthy of your investigation are aeronautical, antitrust, atomic energy, insurance, negligence and compensation, local government, mineral and natural resources, public utility, space, real estate, securities and exchange, zoning, civil rights, constitutional, urban affairs, and environmental.

There are many additional specialty areas that could be added to this list, and even then the list would still be far from complete. Each year brings new laws and new situations to our country and the world, and with these new laws comes the need for lawyers specializing in the particular field. As one practicing woman lawyer noted, "There are so many facets of law, there is bound to be one you especially like. If there isn't one now, just wait a few days and there probably will be one."

6

Every Day
Is Different,
Exciting, Rewarding

A series of phones keep ringing. When one of them is answered, another starts ringing. There's plenty of action. The woman behind the desk is trying to free her sandwich from the lunch bag with one hand while taking notes with the other. The telephone is cradled between her ear and shoulder. A single earring sits on her desk. There's excitement in the air. The attorney seems quite pleased as she says into the phone, "That's O.K. Don't worry about my lunch . . . it will wait. I'm here to help you."

This is typical of a few minutes in the busy day of an attorney. That is, if anything is typical. So many different things happen in the course of a day that there is no way we can imagine a typical one. Instead of imagining, let's see for ourselves by tagging along with a successful lawyer as she goes full tilt on her "typical" day.

The clock radio starts playing at exactly 6:00 A.M.. Both husband and wife lie still, listening to the early-morning news. There's a groan after the previous night's baseball scores are announced and another after the weather report. As soon as the second groan has subsided, two teen-age children appear in the doorway, mumble something that sounds a bit like "good morning," and then sprint for the bathrooms. With four people and two bathrooms, there is usually a certain amount of jockeying for position. The family is now fully "in action" and will remain that way until all members leave—each to a different destination: the mother to her law office, the father to his college teaching position, and the children to junior and senior high school.

There isn't much talking as each family member dresses and does his or her previously assigned housekeeping chores. Then the table is set, coffee "put up," toast made, and eggs scrambled. Breakfast is neither leisurely nor rushed—it might be described as businesslike. There's some pleasant chatter, a little teen-age bickering, and a few parental warnings. At 7:45 everyone pitches in to "do" the kitchen and then the exodus begins. At the sound of a car horn, the senior high student yells, "Oh, I'm late, I'm going to miss my bus," grabs lunch and books and rushes out of the door. Mom, with one smooth motion, picks up her lunch, her purse, and attaché case and is out of the door to the waiting car. Father checks out his briefcase, adding and subtracting papers and books. Satisfied that he has everything, he sits down at the kitchen table with another cup of hot coffee, spreads out the morning newspaper and begins to read it. By the time he gets to the sports pages, the junior high bus comes and the junior high student goes. About ten minutes later the maid arrives and dad knows that's his signal to pack up and get going.

Arriving at her office a bit before 8:30, the lawyer gets right down to business. She checks the mail and then glances over her calendar. The next few minutes are spent getting things started and organized for the day. The secretaries come in, pick up their typing and other assignments and go to their desks. By 9:00 the office is in full swing and the phones start ringing. At 9:05 the lawyer calls one of the secretaries and makes the first of many changes in her calendar for the day—an unexpected trip to the hospital to check on one of her clients. Her client, an elderly lady, had appointed the attorney to be her legal guardian since she had no relatives. The nursing home in which the woman lived was calling to request permission to transfer the client to the hospital. The woman had suffered a stroke while walking upstairs and had fallen down the flight of stairs. The attorney granted permission for the transfer and told the caller she would meet her client at the hospital "to make certain that everything is taken care of and she gets the best of everything."

She buzzes one secretary and details the change in plans: "Call Mrs. ——— and tell her we'll have to see her tomorrow morning instead of today. Tell her it was an emergency, but don't go into any detail. Then call Mr. ——— and tell him I expect to make the 10 o'clock closing, but might be a few minutes late." She then calls her other secretary, Daniel, and both head for the car. As we drive toward the hospital, the lawyer explains about her male secretary, who also serves as her chauffeur and guard.

D. X. Fenten

Real estate closings involve double-checking the premises and contracts before new homeowners sign and "take title"

"It's not safe for *anyone*, let alone a woman, to go into some of the neighborhoods I go into for real estate closing. After all, I'm usually carrying other people's money. I never thought too much about the danger attached to being a lawyer, but lately things are just not the same. I recently went back to my law school for a "guest lecture shot" and was appalled at the way the neighborhood had deteriorated. They had just had several incidents there—one young man was killed at noontime as he was standing on a street corner, because he didn't have a cigarette.

"We always figure tragedies happen to other people and not to us. So I didn't think too much about the possible danger. But, once I had a closing in a rather bad neighborhood which should have been finished long before nightfall, but wasn't. When we finally completed the arrangements, long after dark, I was paid in cash, and left the building. I had to walk quite a distance through city streets and didn't like it one bit. I didn't know who might have seen this man give me the cash or who might have known he was going to a closing or anything else. All I knew was that I was all alone and I was scared. That was the last time I went anywhere without a male chauffeur. Now, whenever I complete a transaction, the car is waiting for me right outside the door and off we go."

Arriving at the hospital, the lawyer quickly checks on the location of her client and then goes upstairs to "see for myself." Though it is not visiting hours at the hospital, she is given the red carpet treatment by the hospital administrator, a close friend for many years. As they walk and talk, the lawyer explains that she is the patient's legal guardian. She tells the administrator that she wants her client to get the "best of everything" and to send all bills to her office. After a few minutes the lawyer returns to the hospital lobby, checks in with her office, and once again heads for the car.

"People don't realize that lawyers can have emergency calls very much like a doctor can. It's true that we don't get them in the middle of the night as often as a doctor does, but we do get them. For example, one night about a year ago I got a call at three o'clock in the morning from one of my clients. She had been called by the police, who told her to come to the hospital immediately—her son had been in an automobile accident and wasn't expected to live very long. My client was calling me from the hospital where she found that it wasn't her son at all that had been hurt. Her car had been stolen by a boy with the same first name. When she called me she was still very upset and didn't know what to do. She had also just learned that the boy was too young to drive, was drunk, and had a girl with him in the car who was also badly hurt. She didn't know what her responsibilities were in this situation or what had to be done.

"By the time I arrived at the hospital, the situation had become even more difficult. My client had refused to sign a complaint against the boy. She said she didn't want him to die with that on his record, and since he wasn't expected to live until morning, why go through with signing a complaint? At that point the police served her with a summons for allowing an unlicensed driver to drive her car. It was a real hair-raising experience and took the rest of the night to straighten out. That's what happens to a lawyer in general practice. Though I don't usually handle accident cases, this was an exception. If one of my clients has a problem, I won't turn my back on him when he is in a nasty situation. Especially in the middle of the night when he needs someone to turn to. You just get yourself up, get organized, and help out every way you can."

There are pleasantries exchanged when the lawyer arrives at the site of the real estate closing. She is representing a small company that has prospered and is now about to take title to a larger home office building. After about an hour of "small print reading" there is an exchange of checks, contract-signing, and handshaking all around. She wishes her client the best of luck and heads, once again, back to the car.

Arriving back at her office a bit after 12 o'clock, she begins to attack the lunch bag while answering the phone and taking notes. She gets as far as removing the sandwich from the bag but is stopped by another phone call before she can open the aluminum foil wrapping. Another "emergency." An elderly client is not feeling well and is panicking, decides he wants to change his will. His doctors tell him it's nothing to worry about, that it's only a virus, but he's sure he knows better. He wants some changes made in his will and he wants them made *today*. The lawyer notes the changes the client wants on her pad and hands it to her secretary. She sits back in her chair for a few minutes and relaxes, telling us, between bites, about the wonderful new automatic typewriter that will be used to produce the new will.

"Much of the work you turn out—wills and such—are not original creations every time. Once you have drawn up several wills and gotten a pattern established

—the opening, closing, and intermediate clauses—you know pretty much what you want to say in each will. Of course, there will be somebody who comes in who wants something out of the ordinary, so you write the clause. But what we have done is to put the major things that appear in almost every will on a magnetic card. Now, every time I want to dictate a will, instead of writing the whole thing out, or, as some lawyers do, say, 'Get Mary Hones's will . . . and copy paragraph three,' . . . I've got a book and we just say copy page one clause one, page two clause four, etc. That's how we do our real estate contracts, our wills, much of our estate work, even some of our letters to heirs (form things that just alert them to the arrival of a court paper). All these are programmed so they don't have to be done individually, every time. We have our separation agreements, our corporate work, corporate minutes, bylaws, and all that sort of thing all on the machine. When something must be drawn up, all I have to do is call out what I want by page number. The appropriate cards are put into the automatic typewriter, and it does the rest. It's really just like programming a computer. A will used to take me one hour to write and the girl three to four hours to type. Now she can do at least five or six wills a day. That sort of thing could never be done before, and I don't even have to check the will, because, except for the person's name, address, and amounts, and so on, I know that it's right. I don't have to check every typewritten word . . . only the part that has been added. It's a great time-saver and is a lot more accurate. It often allows me to be in at least two places at the same time."

She gives instructions to her secretary concerning the

"dying" man's will and goes back into her office to await her afternoon appointments. Each client is given as much time as necessary. As the last one leaves, she packs her attaché case and, with Daniel, heads for an appearance in court. It's a divorce case in which she represents the plaintiff. She arrives at court, waits an interminable amount of time for the case to be called, and when it finally is called, finds that the defendant has gained a delay in the proceedings.

Annoyed at the waste of time, she goes back to her office and works at her desk until 5:30, when she heads for home.

Each day, she says, is "one hundred percent different, exciting, and rewarding." There are some things she does or has done every week, but aside from these, no two days are alike. Every Monday morning she takes off to have her hair done. "Doctors take off Wednesday, male lawyers play golf on Saturday, and I have my hair done on Monday." Twice a week (the same days each week) a woman comes into the law office to do the accounting work for the lawyer's estates and trusts and to file books and maintain the office's up-to-date law library. "We get new sheets weekly and it's very difficult to keep up with all this stuff. She does some of the skimming for me and brings out the highlights of any major changes in fields in which I'm working. Then I can read the specific cases in depth and store the information away in my mind until I need it."

Her evenings at home are similar to those of most people. Dinner with the family at which they chat and discuss the events of the day is followed by some television and some professional reading. Time is spent

D. X. Fenten

Each client is given as much time as his problems and questions require, no matter how minor the case, though it may mean grabbing a snack in the middle of a conference . . .

. . . or putting in extra hours

making notes on things to be accomplished tomorrow, while her husband makes his own notes on tomorrow's classes. Some evenings there may be a meeting, professional or community; other evenings a school function. At 11 P.M. they watch the news, and, when it's over, set the alarm and go to sleep.

It has been a very long but very rewarding day. The lawyer has not neglected her family, her husband, or her clients. They have each shared in her exciting day and each has been helped in one way or another. That, she says, is what makes it all really worthwhile—"You've got to want to help people to be a lawyer. As long as I can help my clients and enjoy my husband and family, well, I guess all's well in my world."

7
All at the Same Time

Man for the field and woman for the hearth:
Man for the sword and for the needle she:
Man with the head and woman with the heart:
Man to command and woman to obey;
All else confusion. . . .

Tennyson's sentiments may have been fine in his day, but poetry has changed, times have changed, and so have women. Women want to work, women like to work, women should and do work. They work at all sorts of jobs and have enviable records. In addition to their away-from-home jobs, many are married, have children, and run a household.

Can a woman be a good lawyer, a good wife, and a good mother all at the same time? Should a young woman interested in a career in the legal profession have to make a decision long before she gets "involved"? Which should she choose to be—an unmarried lawyer, a married lawyer, a married lawyer with children? Or, should she "chuck it all"—chuck the whole lawyer bit, in favor of marriage, a home, and children?

"I have encountered some difficulties because of people refusing to believe that I am serious about the practice of law since I have chosen to accept the responsibilities of a house and three small children. While it is true that I do need to limit my hours at the office, I can be flexible in my schedule and I do consider myself a competent attorney, interested and challenged by the law. I feel that I offer certain special attitudes and legal abilities that are enhanced by my experience as a woman. I feel no need to apologize for being a woman and for accepting traditional female responsibilities—in fact I like it."

"I have been pleasantly surprised to find how much of a practice I would be able to retain practicing from my home. As a general rule, I refuse all cases that might involve a court contest. My practice continues to be very general in nature, revolving around the legal problems of individuals and families."

"I do know that with a family, I like my present position because I don't have a lot of overtime and can devote my hours away from work to my family."

These words are from three successful women lawyers who double as wives, mothers, and homemakers; evidence that a career, a home, and a family can go together and prosper. However, as we indicated in the last chapter, this kind of situation calls for a team effort. It cannot be a one-woman or a one-man kind of setup. Cooperation, understanding, and plenty of shirt-sleeve help are essential if the career is to grow and prosper and the marriage is to become stronger and more devoted.

The image of a Sir Galahad, appearing in your life astride a white horse, is fine for romantic novels out of the Middle Ages. In modern America, a good marriage partner must have a lot more than good looks, pleasant manners, and the ability to ride a horse.

This is not to suggest that you shop for a husband as you would shop for furniture or appliances. If you can define "love" and can choose the right partner that way, go right ahead. But don't get caught with that old cliché, "Love is blind." You had better select your mate with your eyes wide open, because your mate, the mate of a woman lawyer, has got to be something special. He must be helper, companion, and partner in every sense of the word. He must be willing to wash dishes, cook meals, and when the time comes, change diapers. He must be very secure to do these things—secure enough in his own career and in his own mind to be able to accept his role as a partner and not feel that the "man must be king," nor that he is henpecked for sharing these chores and responsibilities. He must truly and deeply believe that his wife is entitled just as much as he is to be fulfilled at the office as well as at home and that, working as a team, they can both be whole happy people. On the question of ego, one long-time practicing woman doctor, wife, mother, and grandmother summarized the requirement: "The husband of a professional woman must be sufficiently confident of himself that he can accept his wife's profession without threat to his own ego."

D. X. Fenten

Marriage must be a partnership for a professional woman. Here a husband and wife team have set up joint law offices in a small suburban town

D. X. Fenten

Another husband and wife law team, specializing in criminal cases, check records in a courthouse file. As a rule each handles his own cases

It would appear that mixing marriage and career can be successfully accomplished, but not without effort. Success in marriage, as success in anything, doesn't just come, it must be worked at. Husband and wife must work at it together, starting with the day they become a team. The question that then comes to mind is: When should that day come? Should you plan on getting married after college, after law school, or after entrance into the profession?

If any planning of these matters can really take place, the best answer to these questions is: There is no single answer that will cover even a small fraction of the possible situations. Psychologists, marriage counselors, and clergymen agree that they cannot agree on one single answer to this complex, very personal question. And when they do arrive at an answer, they must qualify it so much as to make it meaningless.

When a couple marry before either is working in a career situation, there are many interesting and little-thought-of advantages and disadvantages. First and foremost of the problems is the financial one. It takes lots of money to go through law school, and with neither partner working at a high-paying job, this is the time most young couples find out whether they can live on love, or whether two people can live as cheaply as one. Financial problems place great strains on young marriages. However, one recognized advantage of young marriages is realized if both partners know they will have to share everything—good times as well as bad—and use the beginning years to learn, to try, and to grow stronger together. Because neither is set in time-formed ways, both can compromise and give and take until the best road for both is finally found.

Lawyers who marry when they are a bit older and

more settled in their ways generally find that with an understanding spouse each one can continue to do his or her own thing, while showing the mate similar consideration. Here too there must be continual compromise so that each individual remains an individual and the personal and career demands of each are met without unnecessary friction.

It is important to note that unless a careful character analysis is done on a prospective lawyer's prospective husband, the chances of successfully combining career and marriage are greatly strained. The "right guy" to marry a woman lawyer must be "right" in many more ways than if he chooses to marry a noncareer woman.

We hear much said about the problems of running an office and a home, of maintaining a full-time job and a full-time home. One professional woman pointed out the outmoded traditions that traumatize a woman considering a career. She says, "Consider tradition in terms of a woman's life today.

"Less than one hundred years ago a woman was continuously occupied with the preparation of food, the sewing of garments, the heating of the home, and the care of the offspring. She usually had many children and even more pregnancies. Childbirth was a fearsome time. Often the baby died, and sometimes the mother.

"Now we live in draft-free houses where the furnace clicks on and off in the winter, where the rooms light up with the flick of a switch, and where the refrigerator-freezer houses all the food. There are stores bulging with ready-made meals and with ready-to-wear clothes, and most middle-class homes have all the cooking and cleaning gadgets ever invented. One half day of weekly cleaning keeps the house in good shape. One or two weekly visits to the supermarket refill the refrigerator, and a few shopping trips when the seasons change keep the children in clothes and shoes.

"And women have few children. In an overpopulated world, repeated motherhood becomes a dubious virtue. Thus over a very short period of time we have removed or at least greatly reduced a woman's time-honored functions in the home. But at the same time we have not encouraged her to develop into different avenues. Bound by centuries of tradition, we continue to live as if nothing had changed."

Times have changed radically. With all these changes have come some agreement among professional women on the questions of running a home and an office. They agree that running both is difficult, but can be done. To do a good job in both areas, "a woman has to be a good manager, be comfortably able to delegate responsibility, and along with the gratifications, not feel overly drained by meeting the needs of husband, children, clients, and household help."

All agree that household help is essential for a full-time working mother. One practicing woman attorney suggests having more than one baby-sitter on tap and employing cleaning help which is separate from the baby-sitting help. She suggests to other mother-lawyers, "The most important thing is to build a solid base for the children in the beginning. I spent all my extra time with the children when they were young. I can draw on that now.

"My kids know that if there's a Christmas program in school, I'm there. I haven't missed one yet."

She recalls how a federal judge once changed a trial schedule so she wouldn't have to cancel her daughter's birthday party.

"I think my colleagues respected the fact that my kids meant so much to me."

Some women spend a few years at home when their children are very small and then return to their chosen profession. Others continue to work in the law, but at home. This frequently is satisfactory, since hanging out a shingle on one's home to practice law predates most of the modern large law practices. Here too, there are several sides of the picture. One attorney who practices at home while her children are small feels, among other reasons, that she likes knowing she can go upstairs between appointments if a child is sick. Another feels that it is important for her children to be able to speak to her between clients if they want. A third, on the other hand, feels it has somewhat of a constraining effect on her two children, because she insists they not get into loud fights or make a lot of noise while she is having office hours. Up until fairly recently she had an office in a professional building but now practices at home.

The possibilities and the problems for the practicing lawyer-wife-mother are virtually limitless. The three careers, however, can and do go together. In most instances a lawyer in private practice can "call her own tune" on hours, place of practice, and limits on clients. There aren't too many emergency calls in the middle of the night, and there isn't too much overtime work. Many legal matters—briefing, research, and others—can be accomplished just as well and just as easily at home as at an office.

It would seem that if you have "the guts" to be a lawyer and the broad shoulders to be a mother, you have just about all you need to be both. After all, women lawyers are special people to begin with. Married women lawyers are even more so; they work hard in all three of their worlds and, in almost all cases, succeed in all three.

8
What
the Future Holds

Just as there are two sides to every coin, there are two sides to the question, Is the law a good career field for the future? Some analysts feel that there will be a shortage of lawyers in the future, thus making it an excellent career field to consider. Other analysts, using the same statistics, feel that the rate of law school graduations will far outdistance available legal positions and that there will soon be a glut of lawyers. We can only present some facts, some opinions, and some educated guesses, so that you can have enough information to make your own carefully considered decision.

First, let's see the current situation:

"Lawyers have never had it so good," said *Forbes* magazine in September 1971. Then, in a detailed and revealing article called "The Gilt Edged Profession" the magazine set out to show just how good lawyers have it:

> Of the nation's 325,000 lawyers, more than two-thirds are in private practice. Half of those 236,000 practice

alone, and half have partners. The loners are at the very bottom of the profession, averaging around $18,000 by commonly working ten to 12-hour days. But add to that the pleasures of being your own boss, of not being subject to night or Sunday calls like doctors, or of being merged or economized out of a job as happens to corporate executives.

Lawyers in partnerships get around $27,000, or 50% more than the loners. Normally, the more partners, the more each man makes (though a full 75% of the partnerships consist of two to four men). An ordinary partner in a six-man firm gets $35,000; he gets $45,000 in a nine-man firm and roughly $50,000 to $125,000 in one of the 50 largest firms with 10 to 200 men. Senior partners, of course, make more.

The remaining 90,000 lawyers work for others, about half for government and half for corporations. As a rough guide, government lawyers and ordinary solo practitioners make nearly the same amounts, and in-house company counsel and lower-level partners in large firms are about equal. But it's difficult to generalize. IBM pays former Attorney General Nicholas Katzenbach $125,000 to head its in-house law staff, but Katzenbach's counterpart at Aetna Life gets only something over $50,000.

Concluding their assessment of the situation in the legal profession, this influential business magazine suggests, "Everything that happens in the society and in the economy just seems to make more work for them [lawyers]."

A look at some additional statistics will help put this optimistic view into the proper perspective while raising many questions in your mind as you consider law as a career.

In 1961 there were about 41,500 law students. In 1971 there were 94,500. More than 30,000 new lawyers will be available for practicing each year starting in 1974. There will be fewer than 15,000 job openings each year in "strictly legal" work. By 1985, this country will have at least twice as many lawyers as it has today.

These statistics, from the ABA, make it appear as if there will be many more lawyers in the next ten years than there will be positions in which they can practice. These projections make it especially important that you investigate several possibilities currently being examined by the ABA and the Federal Government that would give many more, if not all, Americans as fair a shake as possible in having legal counsel. If put into effect, these suggestions or variations of these plans would require not only the 30,000 new lawyers a year for the next ten years but perhaps even more than that.

The way society is structured today only a very limited number of people can afford legal counsel in most situations. Legal help costs lots of money, and the poor, the almost-poor, and many members of the middle class simply cannot afford to retain lawyers.

Consider for a moment the plight of the poor and the almost-poor. Because of their financial situation and their downtrodden position in the community (often as minority members) these people are frequently taken advantage of by merchants, credit organizations, landlords, and others. Many find themselves in desperate need of expert legal help. For some of them there are legal defenders and *pro bono publico* ("for the common

Astronomically high case loads in legal aid offices will be helped by increasingly sophisticated equipment, like this microfilm reader, to handle record storage and information retrieval

good") offices that give legal services free or at very low cost. These neighborhood free or almost-free law offices are overworked and understaffed. They really try to give everybody "a little help" and are doing a fine job against overwhelming odds, but they simply cannot stem the tide. Because case loads are astronomically high the attention given to individual clients is understandably low. The result is often only a "better than nothing" situation and many poor people are without any legal aid at all.

Then there are the middle-class Americans who are too poor to afford expert legal advice and "too rich" to get any of the free or almost-free advice available on such a limited scale. An article in *Juris Doctor* magazine explained:

"Equally troubling is the plight of the many millions of Americans who fall outside the narrow monetary qualification for free legal assistance yet are not able to afford satisfactory representation. These are the shopkeepers, the blue-collar workers, the manual workers— all are increasingly angry and frustrated. For members of this group, as well as for the very poor, lawyers and the rule of law enter their lives only defensively and often at the last desperate moment. Barely do these citizens enjoy the benefits of proper legal counseling, even when faced with severe personal or financial problems. Society, in short, has failed to provide a vast number of our fellow citizens with their fair share of the rule of law."

To remedy this situation requires lawyers and money to pay for them. The article suggests several ways to get a "fair share of the rule of law" for all American citizens:

"Funding for neighborhood law offices should be substantially increased and more such offices opened. A government-subsidized lawyer program should be started to assist people who, though able to pay something, lack sufficient funds for adequate legal help when needed. Group practice, legal insurance, and judicare plans all deserve careful consideration. Public awareness of the value of legal assistance should be increased so that people will seek counsel on a preventive basis and come to rely on the law as meaningful to their daily lives."

This will create new, relevant jobs for attorneys and make our society more honest in soliciting participation by *all* its citizens.

Another innovation in the legal profession should be considered because it is an important part of the future lawyer's employment picture. Legalcare or some form of prepaid legal insurance would make lawyer's services available to many, many additional Americans. Available in a few states now, this plan will certainly be made available in more states in the very near future. Modeled after Blue Cross and other successful prepaid medical plans, this type of legal insurance will create many new career opportunities for attorneys. *Forbes* magazine describes the plan and its effect on lawyers:

> Under Legalcare, a member of a union or some other group would pay $5 a month to get basic legal services covering roughly 90% of a member's foreseeable needs, including bankruptcy, divorce, defense in a civil suit— even a full defense for a murder trial. For $10 a month, the member gets even more and can initiate suits; for $13.95, the whole family is covered. What's more,

unions may soon begin demanding Legalcare-type programs. So lawyers could end up costing the individual almost nothing at all. One problem: convincing the public it needs legal services.

What's in these innovations for lawyers? Plenty. Specialization, as doctors discovered long ago, could mean even higher fees. And providing prepaid services could make some lawyers richer (though many ordinary lawyers could lose business). Under Legalcare, for example, $3 of the $5 monthly fee goes to an attorney as a retainer. According to Legalcare consultant Danny R. Jones, one lawyer can handle the routine problems of 3,000 to 5,000 members without much trouble, while collecting $15,000 a month.

Would he be overpaid? Maybe not from the public's point of view, for nothing is more expensive than incompetent legal service.

There will be an increasing demand for attorneys in addition to that caused by the implementation of programs of Legalcare and of legal help for the poor. More and more attorneys will be required to work with people, corporations, and governments in the "regular" or, as one attorney suggested, "really lucrative" parts of the legal profession. Population around the world continues to go up, and with that rise the requirements to regulate it. The more people there are, the closer together they must live, and this creates friction. Regulation is required to prevent the friction if possible and to set out penalties if friction occurs. Lawyers are required at every step along the way to help draft the legislation of regulations, to interpret it to lay people once it is in effect, to adapt it within the framework of current laws and to litigate questions of enforcement.

A look at the other side of the coin shows somewhat of a decrease in lawyer employment possibilities in certain areas in the future. No-fault automobile insurance is operating in many states and is being considered in many others. Under this form of insurance, the insuring companies must pay *all* car accident victims, eliminating the need for litigation and for lawyers except in the extreme cases where a victim has been very badly hurt. No-fault divorce is being talked about and is being considered as a very distinct possibility in the near future. The elimination of these two reasons for court cases, suits, and lawyers will cut deeply into the day-to-day, bread-and-butter activities of many lawyers.

Careful consideration of the possible gains against the possible losses in employment in the legal profession leads one to believe that the gains will be far greater than the losses.

Just as long as people fall in love, marry, and divorce; just as long as people start up and close down businesses; just as long as the government has one hand in your pocket for taxes and tax laws become more and more confusing; just as long as people buy and sell real estate, merchandise, hard goods, and soft goods; and just as long as people are born, live, and die, there will be a continually increasing demand for attorneys. There is little doubt therefore of the necessity for more and more lawyers in the future.

That prediction or calculated guess concerns attorneys—all attorneys, which currently means about 95 percent male and the remainder female. What does the future hold for female lawyers? It holds the same and even better promise for female lawyers as for male lawyers. Times are changing, although slowly. More and more women are becoming visible in the professions and in the crafts and in blue-collar work. And, with very few exceptions, certainly no more or no less than among males, women workers are doing an excellent job. Perhaps the entire situation was summarized best by a labor arbitrator who in ruling against a male who disliked taking orders from a female supervisor said, "Women are taking a bigger part in our society—this is something that we males have to adjust to."

Adjusting to the situation will certainly make life a bit easier for everyone, but it will not really hurry the progress toward equality in the number of male and female lawyers. We can, however, expect other things to be done in the near future that will bring more and more qualified women into the legal profession:

1. Concerted, comprehensive attacks, backed up by facts and figures, will be made on the myths and prejudices toward women in law, using all the media and reaching as many men, women, and especially children as possible.

2. Many law schools will follow the lead of a few "icebreakers" and mount full-fledged recruitment drives aimed at getting more female law students and more female faculty members into the law schools.

3. Since the image of the lawyer has suffered considerably recently because of the scandals in which lawyers were so deeply involved, all of them—male lawyers,

various lawyers groups and associations—will attempt to use improved public relations and education to win men and women into considering law for a career. It is impossible to conceive that there will be any room for a continuation of the blatant sex discrimination in the legal profession as the profession tries to regain the confidence of the American public. After all, the American public that has lost faith in the legal profession is made up of 51 percent women and 49 percent men.

4. Modern living requires modern solutions to everyday problems. We can expect the more "daring" law schools, followed by the slower learners, to change many of their policies toward married students and families. Perhaps the most desirable change would allow the husbands and families of women students to live on the campus. These changes are being made today. Along with these changes we can also expect increases in day care facilities for children and more and better housing on campus, for all students, married or single.

5. On the horizon are special reorientation programs for interviewers—admissions officers, or employment directors—to eliminate the obvious discrimination against women. Unless interviewers ask males the same questions, they will be forbidden to ask a woman student "about her method of birth control, whether she will have children and how they will be cared for."

6. Just as important as the reorientation of interviewers is the reawakening of male faculty members. It won't be long before there are special programs for male faculty members designed to eliminate all the prejudices and needling sex discrimination in the class-

room. No one will admit that these unfortunate "jokes" and bits and pieces of "unintentional" sex discrimination exist in the classroom (or in the courtroom for that matter), but a new look at some old patterns is in the offing and certainly can do no harm, only good.

These are but a few of the suggestions we can expect will be followed as we deliberately attempt to get more women into the legal profession. Of course there are many more, including curriculum flexibility, additional financial aid for law students, changed admissions policies, and the banning of law firms that discriminate against women from interviewing anyone on law school campuses.

What should practicing women lawyers do for themselves and for those who come in the future? And how should they do it? A female researcher writing in the *ABA Journal* suggested:

> Female attorneys, in advising other members of their sex as to the best way of handling sex discrimination, subscribe to two distinct and violently conflicting schools of thought. One group advises open conflict—the other the diplomatic use of tactical weapons and a graceful retreat if necessary.

> Advocates of diplomacy cover a broad spectrum in their approach to sex discrimination. Some say "ignore it." Others say "recognize its existence but work around the problem rather than through it."

> Women in the first group are often so successful in ignoring bias that they actually become a party to discrimination against members of their own sex. During the course of this survey, many women voiced

violent opposition to any study of discriminatory practices in the legal field on the ground that "it is not
healthy to look for prejudice." Others went so far as to
share a generally male aversion toward female attorneys, charging their female colleagues with everything
from incompetence to distorted personalities and unre-
solved aggressive tendencies.

More sympathetic members of the diplomatic group
(representing by far the largest proportion of female
attorneys) recognize the existence of prejudice but
prefer not to launch a direct, offensive attack against its
injustices. Instead, they try to gain acceptance by "not
coming on too strong." "Do a good job but be
inconspicuous about it." "Stay in the background at all
times, convince your male colleagues that your ideas are
really theirs, and never reveal any strong, forthright
opinions" advises a female member of a district attorney's office.

The "fighters" see the "diplomats" as cowardly and
damaging to members of their own sex. "Sex discrimination exists in the legal field because women themselves have been unwilling to break down its barriers,"
charges a dynamic female attorney in private practice.
"Content with the place assigned to them, most women
attorneys docilely accept less pay, less prestige and less
recognition, expending far greater effort than their male
colleagues in the hope of gaining even a minimum of
acceptance." "It's amazing what guff women will take
from men," agrees another. "Social conditioning and
the more practical fear of losing their jobs encourage
women to downgrade themselves. These women are
inviting men to step all over them and, in doing so, are
inflicting a negative image on all female members of
their profession."

The choice between "fighter" and "diplomat" will have to be made by you a lot sooner than you think. You can either force discrimination against women into the open and try to defeat it that way or you can work behind the scenes to try to eliminate it. The choice will be up to you—and it must be made.

Whichever method you choose, you can be certain that lawyers, old and new, know they can no longer discriminate against women with impunity. They can no longer believe that the legal profession is a "special case" and need not heed the antidiscrimination laws. They know they must make legitimate attempts to balance the percentage of males and females in their profession. And they also know they cannot get away with tokenism.

The future holds the promise of smoother roads to legal careers for qualified women. But the question comes up time and time again: How near is that future? Our answer is, Just as close as the next very special woman who goes through all that is necessary to become Ms.—Attorney.

Appendix

AMERICAN LAW SCHOOLS
WITH ADMISSION REQUIREMENTS
AND FINANCIAL INFORMATION

The list that follows contains the names, addresses, and pertinent admission and financial information of law schools in the United States conducting courses at the time of publication. All entries indicate *minimum estimates*.

KEY TO INFORMATION

ABA	American Bar Association
AALS	Association of American Law Schools
State	State Law School accredited
BRSNY	Board of Regents of the State of New York
LSAT	Law School Aptitude Test required
LSDAS	Law School Data Assembly Service required
Tuition	Resident—Person who lives within a state and is required to pay less in tuition at certain publicly supported schools. *All tuition listings are minimum estimates on an annual basis.*

*	School will accept less than a bachelor's degree under exceptional circumstances, but *prefers* 4 years of college.
(Day–Eve)	Full schedule of courses in day and evening hours. Schools without this notation have day schedules only.

DEGREES AWARDED

C.L.U.	Chartered Life Underwriter
C.P.C.U.	Chartered Property Casualty Underwriter
D.C.L.	Doctor of Civil Law
D.J.S.	Doctor of Juridical Science
J.D.	Juris Doctor
J.S.D.	Doctor of the Science of Law
LL.B.	Bachelor of Laws
LL.M.	Masters of Laws
M.A.	Master of Arts
M.B.A.	Master of Business Administration
M.C.J.	Master of Comparative Jurisprudence
M.C.L.	Master of Comparative Law
M.L.T.	Master of Laws in Taxation
M.R.P.	Master of Regional Planning
M.S.–E.H.E.	Master of Science in Environmental Health Engineering
M.Th.	Master of Theology

Akron, University of
   (ABA, State)
School of Law
Akron, Ohio 44325
Degree—J.D. (Day–Eve)
Requirements
   Bachelor's + LSAT-
      LSDAS
   Fall admission only
   Application by March 1
Tuition
   $736—residents
   $828—nonresidents
Other Expenses
   Room, board—approx.
      $1,300
   Books—$150

Alabama, University of
   (ABA, AALS)
School of Law
University, Ala. 35486
Degree—J.D. + M.C.L. +
J.D.-M.B.A.
Requirements
   Bachelor's + LSAT-
      LSDAS
   Fall admission only
   Application by April 1
Tuition
   $710—residents
   $1,220—nonresidents
Other Expenses
   Books—approx. $150

Albany Law School
   (ABA, AALS, BRSNY)
80 New Scotland Ave.

Albany, N.Y. 12208
Degree—J.D.
Requirements
   Bachelor's* + LSAT
   Fall admission only
Tuition
   $2,000

American University
   (ABA, AALS, State)
Washington College of Law
Washington, D.C. 20016
Degree—J.D. (Day–Eve)
Requirements
   Bachelor's + LSAT-
      LSDAS
   Fall admission only
   Application by March 15
Tuition
   $2,190

Arizona, University of
   (ABA, AALS)
College of Law
Tucson, Ariz. 85721
Degree—J.D.
Requirements
   Bachelor's + LSAT
Tuition
   $481—residents
   $1,371—nonresidents
Other Expenses
   Living—approx. $1,200
   Books, etc.—$200

Arizona State University
   (ABA, AALS)
College of Law

Tempe, Ariz. 85281
Degree—J.D.
Requirements
　Bachelor's + LSAT-
　　LSDAS
　Fall admission only
　Application by April 1
Tuition
　$384—residents
　$1,274—nonresidents
Other Expenses
　Living—approx. $1,600

Arkansas, University of
　(ABA, AALS)
School of Law
Fayetteville, Ark. 72701
Degree—J.D. (Eve only)
Requirements
　Bachelor's + LSAT-
　　LSDAS
　Fall admission only
　Application by May 1
Tuition
　$400—residents
　$930—nonresidents
Other Expenses
　Room and board—$950

Baltimore, University of
　(ABA, State)
School of Law
1420 N. Charles St.
Baltimore, Md. 21201
Degree—J.D. (Day–Eve)
Requirements
　Bachelor's + LSAT-
　　LSDAS

Fall admission only
Application by April 5
Tuition
　$1,200

Baylor University
　(ABA, AALS)
School of Law
Waco, Tex. 76703
Degree—J.D.
Requirements
　Degree not required,
　　accepts mature students
　　after 3 years of college
　　(quarter system),
　　classes enter three times
　　a year. Application by
　　Nov. 1 (spring), Feb. 1
　　(summer), March 1
　　(fall)
Tuition
　$1,050
Other Expenses
　Room, board—approx.
　　$1,000

Boston College
　(ABA, AALS)
School of Law
Brighton, Mass. 02135
Degree—J.D.
Requirements
　Bachelor's + LSAT-
　　LSDAS
　Fall admission only
　Application by March 1
Tuition
　$2,450

Percent Women Students
18% and increasing

Boston University
   (ABA, AALS)
School of Law
765 Commonwealth Ave.
Boston, Mass. 02215
Degree—J.D. + M.L.T.
Requirements
   Bachelor's + LSAT-
      LSDAS
   Fall admission only
   Application by March 1
Tuition
   About $2,700
Other Expenses
   Books, supplies, living—
      approx. $2,700
Percent Women Students
   25% and increasing

Brooklyn Law School
   (ABA, BRSNY)
250 Joralemon St.
Brooklyn, N.Y. 11201
Degree—J.D. (Day–Part
   Eve)
Requirements
   Bachelor's + LSAT-
      LSDAS
   Fall admission only
   Application by April 1
Tuition
   $1,500

California, University of,
   Berkeley
   (ABA, AALS)

Boalt Hall School of Law
Berkeley, Calif. 94720
Degree—J.D. + LL.M. +
   J.S.D.
Requirements
   Bachelor's + LSAT
   Application by March 1
Tuition
   $708—residents
   $2,200—nonresidents

California, University of,
   Davis
   (ABA, AALS)
School of Law
Davis, Calif. 95616
Degree—J.D.
Requirements
   Bachelor's + LSAT-
      LSDAS
Tuition
   $670—residents
   $2,170—nonresidents
Other Expenses
   Approx. $3,000
Percent Women Students
   15%

California, University of, Los
   Angeles
   (ABA, AALS)
School of Law
405 Hilgard Ave.
Los Angeles, Calif. 90024
Degree—LL.B. + J.D.
Requirements
   Bachelor's + LSAT-
      LSDAS

Application by March 1
Tuition
    $696—residents
    $2,196—nonresidents

California, University of, San
    Francisco
    (ABA, AALS)
Hastings College of the Law
198 McAllister St.
San Francisco, Calif. 94102
Degree—J.D.
Requirements
    Bachelor's + LSAT
    Fall admission only
    Application by March 1
Tuition
    $660—residents
    $1,800—nonresidents
Percent Women Students
    21% and increasing

California Western Law
    School
    (ABA, AALS, State)
United States International
    University
San Diego, Calif. 92106
Degree—J.D.
Requirements
    Bachelor's + LSAT-
        LSDAS
    Fall admission only
    Application by May 1
Tuition
    $1,800

Other Expenses
    Approx. $3,000
Percent Women Students
    8%

Capital University
    (ABA, State)
Law School
Columbus, Ohio 43209
Degree—J.D. (Day–Eve)
Requirements
    Bachelor's + LSAT-
        LSDAS
    Fall admission only
Tuition
    $2,035
Other Expenses
    $1,075
Percent Women Students
    About 5%

Case Western Reserve
    University
    (ABA, AALS)
Law School
11075 East Blvd.
Cleveland, Ohio 44106
Degree—J.D.
Requirements
    Bachelor's + LSAT-
        LSDAS
    Fall admission only
    Application by May 1
Tuition
    $2,300
Other Expenses
    Room, board, books,
        supplies—$1,700

Catholic University of
America
(ABA, AALS)
Columbus School of Law
Washington, D.C. 20017
Degree—J.D. (Day–Eve) +
J.D.-M.A.
Requirements
Bachelor's + LSAT-
LSDAS
Aug. admission only
Application by May 1
Tuition
$2,200
Other Expenses
Room and board—$1,800
Books and supplies—
approx. $200

Chicago, University of
(ABA, AALS)
The Law School
1111 E. 60th St.
Chicago, Ill. 60637
Degree—J.D. + J.D.-
M.B.A.
Requirements
Bachelor's* + LSAT-
LSDAS
Application by Jan. 1
Tuition
$2,775
Other Expenses
Room, board, etc.—
approx. $2,800

Chicago-Kent College of Law
(ABA, AALS)

Illinois Institute of
Technology
10 N. Franklin St.
Chicago, Ill. 60606
Degree—J.D. (Day–Eve)
Requirements
Bachelor's* + LSAT-
LSDAS
Admission in Sept. or Feb.,
but Sept. preferred
Tuition
$1,320
Other Expenses
Room, board—approx.
$1,100

Cincinnati, University of
(ABA, AALS, State)
College of Law
Cincinnati, Ohio 45221
Degree—J.D.
Requirements
Bachelor's + LSAT-
LSDAS
Application by March 1
Tuition
$780—Cincinnati
residents
$975—Ohio residents
$1,770—nonresidents
Other Expenses
Room and board—$1,750

Cleveland State University
(ABA, AALS, State)
Marshall College of Law
Cleveland, Ohio 44115
Degree—J.D. (Day–Part

Eve) + LL.M. + LL.M-Advocacy + M.C.L.
Requirements
  Bachelor's + LSAT-LSDAS
  Fall admission only
  Application by April 1
Tuition
  $990—residents
  $1,980—nonresidents
Percent Women Students
  Approx. 13%

Colorado, University of
  (ABA, AALS)
School of Law
Boulder, Colo. 80302
Degree—J.D.
Requirements
  Bachelor's + LSAT-LSDAS
  Fall admission only
  Application by Jan. 15
Tuition
  $553—residents
  $1,821—nonresidents
Other Expenses
  Books, living, etc.,—
    approx. $2,000
Percent Women Students
  21%

Columbia University
  (ABA, AALS)
School of Law
435 W. 116th St.
New York, N.Y. 10027

Degree—J.D. + LL.M. +
  J.S.D.
Requirements
  Bachelor's + LSAT-LSDAS
  Fall admission only
  Application by March 1
Tuition
  $3,000
Other Expenses
  Fees—$80; room and
    board—$1,550
  Books and misc.—$600
Percent Women Students
  20%

Connecticut, University of
  (ABA, AALS)
School of Law
West Hartford, Conn. 06117
Degree—J.D. (Day–Eve)
Requirements
  Bachelor's + LSAT-LSDAS
  Application by Feb. 1
Tuition
  $650—residents
  $1,150—nonresidents
Other Expenses
  Room, board—approx.
    $1,800

Cornell University
  (ABA, AALS)
The Law School
Ithaca, N.Y. 14850
Degree—J.D. + LL.M. +

J.S.D. + Special Programs
in Business, Industrial
Relations, Regional
Planning
Requirements
    Bachelor's + LSAT-
        LSDAS
    Fall admission only
    Application by March 1
Tuition
    $2,800
Other Expenses
    Room, board—approx.
        $1,550
    Books and supplies—$200

Creighton University
    (ABA, AALS)
School of Law
Omaha, Nebr. 68131
Degree—J.D.
Requirements
    Bachelor's + LSAT-
        LSDAS
    Admission in Aug. only
    Application by April 7
Tuition
    $2,000
Other Expenses
    Room, board—approx.
        $1,050

Denver, University of
    (ABA, AALS, BRSNY)
College of Law
200 W. 14th Ave.
Denver, Colo. 80204
Degree—J.D. (Day–Eve)

Requirements
    Bachelor's + LSAT-
        LSDAS
    Fall admission only
Tuition
    $2,550
Other Expenses
    Room and board—$1,200
    Books—$150
Percent Women Students
    Approx. 10%

DePaul University
    (ABA, AALS)
College of Law
25 E. Jackson Blvd.
Chicago, Ill. 60604
Degree—J.D. (Day–Eve)
Requirements
    Bachelor's + LSAT-
        LSDAS
    Application by March 1
Tuition
    $1,650
Other Expenses
    Room—$1,320
Percent Women Students
    20%

Detroit College of Law
    (ABA, AALS)
136 E. Elizabeth
Detroit, Mich. 48201
Degree—J.D. (Day–Eve)
Requirements
    Bachelor's + LSAT
    Fall application by Jan. 1,
        spring by June 1

Tuition
 $1,000
Other Expenses
 Books and supplies—$250

Detroit, University of
 (ABA, AALS)
School of Law
651 E. Jefferson
Detroit, Mich. 48226
Degree—J.D. (Day–Eve)
Requirements
 Bachelor's + LSAT
 Fall admission only
 Application by March 15
Tuition
 $1,700
Other Expenses
 Room and board—$1,700
 Books and supplies—$175

Dickinson School of Law
 (ABA, AALS, BRSNY)
Carlisle, Pa. 17013
Degree—J.D. + M.C.L.
Requirements
 Bachelor's + LSAT +
  two recommendations
Tuition
 $1,200—residents
 $1,400—nonresidents
Other Expenses
 Room—$360–$410
 Misc. fees—average $50
Percent Women Students
 Very small but increasing

Drake University
 (ABA, AALS)
Law School
Des Moines, Iowa 50311
Degree—J.D. + J.D.-
 M.B.A. + J.D.-C.L.U. +
 J.D.-M.A.
Requirements
 Bachelor's + LSAT-
  LSDAS
 Summer and fall
  admission
 Application by May 1
Tuition
 $2,120
Other Expenses
 Room, board—approx.
  $1,250

Duke University
 (ABA, AALS)
School of Law
Durham, N.C. 27706
Degree—LL.B. + J.D. +
 M.D.-J.D. + M.B.A.-J.D.
Requirements
 Bachelor's* + LSAT-
  LSDAS
 Fall admission only
 Application by Jan. 1
Tuition
 $2,350
Other Expenses
 Books, living, etc.—
  approx. $4,000
Percent Women Students
 Approx. 10%

Duquesne University
(ABA, AALS)
School of Law
600 Forbes Ave.
Pittsburgh, Pa. 15219
Degree—J.D. (Day–Eve)
Requirements
Bachelor's + LSAT-
LSDAS
Fall admission only
Application by April 1
Tuition
$1,800

Emory University
(ABA, AALS)
School of Law
Atlanta, Ga. 30322
Degree—J.D.
Requirements
Bachelor's + LSAT
Fall admission only
Application by April 1
Tuition
$2,250
Other Expenses
Living—approx. $1,800
Books—$200
Percent Women Students
15%

Florida State University
(ABA, AALS)
College of Law
Tallahassee, Fla. 32306
Degree—J.D. + J.D.-
M.B.A + J.D.-M.S. in
Public Administration or

International Affairs
Requirements
Bachelor's + LSAT
Fall admission only
Tuition
$720—residents
$1,770—nonresidents
Other Expenses
Approx. $2,250
Percent Women Students
Approx. 4%

Florida, University of
(ABA, AALS, BRSNY)
Holland Law Center
Gainesville, Fla. 32601
Degree—J.D.
Requirements
Bachelor's + LSAT
Application by April 1
(fall), Nov. 1 (spring)
Tuition
$720—residents
$1,770—nonresidents
Other Expenses
Room and board—$1,900
Books and supplies—$250

Fordham University
(ABA, AALS)
School of Law
140 W. 62d St.
New York, N.Y. 10023
Degree—J.D. (Day–Eve)
Requirements
Bachelor's + LSAT-
LSDAS

Fall admission only
Application by April 1
Tuition
$2,400
Other Expenses
Books—approx. $125
Percent Women Students
9% and increasing

Georgetown University
  (ABA, AALS, BRSNY)
Law Center
600 New Jersey Ave., N.W.
Washington, D.C. 20001
Degree—J.D. (Day–Eve) +
  M.C.L. + LL.M. (also in
  Taxation and Patents) +
  J.S.D. + D.C.L.
Requirements
  Bachelor's + LSAT-
    LSDAS
  Fall admission only
  Application by March 1
Tuition
  $2,500
Other Expenses
  Room, board, etc.—
    $2,500
Percent Women Students
  11% and increasing

George Washington
  University
  (ABA, AALS)
National Law Center
305 Bacon Hall
2000 H St., N.W.
Washington, D.C., 20006

Degree—J.D. (Day–Eve) +
  LL.M. + M.C.L. +
  J.S.D.
Requirements
  Bachelor's + LSAT-
    LSDAS
  Fall admission only
Tuition
  $2,200
  Fees—$75
Other Expenses
  Room and board—$1,500

Georgia, University of
  (ABA, AALS, State)
School of Law
Athens, Ga. 30601
Degree—J.D. + LL.M. +
  J.D.-M.B.A.
Requirements
  Bachelor's + LSAT-
    LSDAS
  Fall admission only
Tuition
  $639—residents
  $1,359—nonresidents
Other Expenses
  Room and board—$925
  Books and supplies—$200

Golden Gate College
  (ABA, State)
School of Law
536 Mission
San Francisco, Calif. 94105
Degree—J.D. (Day–Eve) +
  J.D.-M.B.A.

Requirements
  Bachelor's* + LSAT-
    LSDAS
  Fall admission only
  Application by May 1
Tuition
  $1,440
Percent Women Students
  Approx. 34%

Gonzaga University
  (ABA)
School of Law
E. 600 Sharp Ave.
Spokane, Wash. 99202
Degree—J.D. (Day–Eve)
Requirements
  Bachelor's + LSAT
  Fall admission only
Tuition
  $1,400
Other Expenses
  Room and board—$1,000

Harvard University
  (ABA, AALS)
Law School
Cambridge, Mass. 02138
Degree—J.D. + LL.M. +
  J.S.D.
Requirements
  Bachelor's + LSAT-
    LSDAS
  Fall admission only
  Application by March 1
Tuition
  $2,400
  Fees—$150

Other Expenses
  Approx. $2,500

Hofstra University
  (ABA)
School of Law
Hempstead, N.Y. 11550
Degree—J.D.
Requirements
  Bachelor's + LSAT-
    LSDAS
  Fall admission only
  Application by April 15
Tuition
  $2,300
  Fees—$40
Other Expenses
  $1,300
  Books—approx. $150
Percent Women Students
  20%

Houston, University of
  (ABA, AALS)
College of Law
Cullen Blvd.
Houston, Tex. 77004
Degree—J.D. (Day–Eve)
Requirements
  Bachelor's + LSAT-
    LSDAS
  Fall admission only
  Application by May 1
Tuition
  $120—residents
  $1,200—nonresidents

Other Expenses
   Room and board—$1,500
   Books—$150

Howard University
   (ABA, AALS)
Washington, D.C. 20001
Degree—J.D.-M.C.J.
Requirements
   Bachelor's + LSAT +
      testimonials
Tuition
   Approx. $600
Other Expenses
   Room, board—approx.
      $1,000

Idaho, University of
   (ABA, AALS)
College of Law
Moscow, Idaho 83843
Degree—J.D.
Requirements
   Bachelor's + LSAT-
      LSDAS
   Fall admission only
Tuition
   $550 mandatory fees
      (health, etc.)—
      residents
   $1,350 (tuition plus fees)
      —nonresidents

Illinois, University of
   (ABA, AALS)
College of Law
Champaign, Ill. 61820

Degree—J.D. + LL.M. +
   J.S.D.
Requirements
   Bachelor's + LSAT-
      LSDAS
   Application by March 15
Tuition
   $496—residents
   $1,486—nonresidents
Other Expenses
   Fees—$95; books, etc.—
      $215
   Room and board—approx.
      $1,200; misc.—$524

Indiana University
   (ABA, AALS)
School of Law
Bloomington, Ind. 47401
Degree—J.D. + LL.M. +
   J.D.-M.B.A. + Ph.D. in
   Law
Requirements
   Bachelor's + LSAT-
      LSDAS
   Application by March 1
Tuition
   Approx. $780—residents
   Approx. $1,800—
      nonresidents
Other Expenses
   Approx. $1,500
Percent Women Students
   10%

Indiana University
   (ABA, AALS)
Indianapolis Law School

735 W. New York St.
Indianapolis, Ind. 46202
Degree—J.D. (Day–Eve)
Requirements
  Bachelor's + LSAT-
    LSDAS
  Application by April 15
Tuition
  $765—residents
  $1,760—nonresidents
Other Expenses
  Approx. $1,800
  Books—$200
Percent Women Students
  Approx. 7%

Iowa, University of
  (ABA, AALS)
College of Law
Iowa City, Iowa 52240
Degree—J.D. + J.D.-M.A.
  + J.D.-Ph.D.
Requirements
  Bachelor's + LSAT
  Application by May 1
Tuition
  $710—residents
  $1,270—nonresidents
Other Expenses
  $1,600
  Books—$140
Percent Women Students
  12%

John Marshall Law School
  (ABA, State)
315 S. Plymouth Court
Chicago, Ill. 60604

Degree—J.D. (Day–Part
  Eve) + LL.M.
Requirements
  Bachelor's* + LSAT-
    LSDAS
  Feb. and Sept. admission
  Application by Dec. 1 and
    May 15
Tuition
  $1,540

Kansas, University of
  (ABA, AALS)
School of Law
Lawrence, Kans. 66044
Degree—J.D. + J.D.-
  M.B.A.
Requirements
  Bachelor's + LSAT-
    LSDAS
  Application by March 15
    (summer), May 15
    (fall)
Tuition
  $563—residents
  $1,153—nonresidents
Other Expenses
  Books and supplies—$200

Kentucky, University of
  (ABA, AALS)
College of Law
Lexington, Ky. 40506
Degree—J.D.
Requirements
  Bachelor's + LSAT-
    LSDAS
  Application by March 1

Tuition
    $405—residents
    $1,120—nonresidents
Other Expenses
    Room and board—$2,200

Lewis and Clark College
    (ABA, State)
Northwestern School of Law
10015 S. W. Terwilliger
    Blvd.
Portland, Oreg. 97219
Degree—J.D. (Day–Eve)
Requirements
    Bachelor's + LSAT-
        LSDAS
    Fall admission only
    Application by March 15
Tuition
    $1,900
    Fees—approx. $65
Other Expenses
    Books—average $180

Louisiana State University
    (ABA, AALS, BRSNY)
The Law School
Baton Rouge, La. 70803
Degree—J.D. + LL.M. +
    M.C.L.
Requirements
    Bachelor's + LSAT-
        LSDAS
    Fall admission only
Tuition
    $630—residents
    $1,140—nonresidents

Louisville, University of
    (ABA, AALS, BRSNY)
School of Law
Louisville, Ky. 40208
Degree—J.D. (Day–Part
    Eve)
Requirements
    Bachelor's + LSAT-
        LSDAS
    Fall admission only
    Application by Jan. 15
Tuition
    $1,050—residents
    $1,950—nonresidents
Other Expenses
    $2,200

Loyola University
    (ABA, AALS)
School of Law
41 E. Pearson St.
Chicago, Ill. 60611
Degree—J.D. (Day–Eve)
Requirements
    Bachelor's* + LSAT-
        LSDAS
    Fall admission only
    Application by March 1
Tuition
    $1,650

Loyola University
    (ABA, AALS, State,
        BRSNY)
School of Law
1440 W. Ninth St.
Los Angeles, Calif. 90015
Degree—J.D. (Day–Eve)

Requirements
   Bachelor's
Tuition
   $2,275

Loyola University
   (ABA, AALS)
School of Law
New Orleans, La. 70118
Degree—J.D. (Day–Eve)
Requirements
   Bachelor's* + LSAT-
      LSDAS
   Application by April1
Tuition
   $1,700

Maine, University of
   (ABA, AALS)
School of Law
246 Deering Ave.
Portland, Maine 04102
Degree—J.D.
Requirements
   Bachelor's + LSAT-
      LSDAS
   Fall admission only
   Application by Feb. 15
Tuition
   $550—residents
   $1,650—nonresidents
Other Expenses
   Approx. $2,300
Percent Women Students
   Approx. 8%

Marquette University
   (ABA, AALS)

Law School
1103 W. Wisconsin Ave.
Milwaukee, Wis. 53233
Degree—J.D.
Requirements
   Bachelor's + LSAT
Tuition
   $1,980

Maryland, University of
   (ABA, AALS)
School of Law
500 W. Baltimore St.
Baltimore, Md. 21201
Degree—J.D. (Day–Eve)
Requirements
   Bachelor's + LSAT-
      LSDAS
   Fall admission only
   Application by March 1
Tuition
   $581—residents
   $1,181—nonresidents
Other Expenses
   Approx. $3,000

Memphis State University
   (ABA)
School of Law
Memphis, Tenn. 38111
Degree—J.D. (Day–Eve)
Requirements
   Bachelor's + LSAT
   Fall admission only
   Application by Jan. 1
Tuition
   $378—residents
   $918—nonresidents

Other Expenses
Room, board—approx.
$1,000
Books and supplies—$150
Percent Women Students
5%

Mercer University
(ABA, AALS, State)
Walter F. George School of
Law
1400 Coleman Ave.
Macon, Ga. 31207
Degree—J.D.
Requirements
Bachelor's* + LSAT-
LSDAS
Tuition
$1,500
Other Expenses
Room—approx. $450
Percent Women Students
Very, very small

Miami, University of
(ABA, AALS)
School of Law
Coral Gables, Fla. 33124
Degree—J.D. (Day–Eve) +
M.C.L. + LL.M. (in
Inter-American Law,
International Law,
Taxation, and Ocean Law)
Requirements
Bachelor's + LSAT-
LSDAS
Fall admission only
Application by Feb. 1

Tuition
$2,300

Michigan, University of
(ABA, AALS)
Law School
312 Hutchins Hall
Ann Arbor, Mich. 48104
Degree—J.D.
Requirements
Bachelor's + LSAT-
LSDAS
Application by April 1
Tuition
$950—residents
$2,400—nonresidents
Other Expenses
Books, supplies—approx.
$175
Percent Women Students
Approx. 5%

Minnesota, University of
(ABA, AALS)
Law School
Minneapolis, Minn. 55455
Degree—J.D.
Requirements
Bachelor's + LSAT-
LSDAS
Fall admission only
Application by March 1
Tuition
$756—residents
$1,641—nonresidents
Other Expenses
Room, board, and misc.—
approx. $2,200

Mississippi, University of
(ABA, AALS)
School of Law
University, Miss. 38677
Degree—J.D. + LL.M. +
M.C.L. + J.S.D. +
Master of Marine Law
and Science
Requirements
Bachelor's + LSAT-
LSDAS
Application by March 1
(summer—nonresi-
dent); April 1 (resi-
dent); March 1 (fall—
nonresident); June 15
(resident)
Tuition
$706—residents
$1,306—nonresidents
Other Expenses
Rooms—approx. $260
Books—approx. $160

Missouri, University of,
Columbia
(ABA, AALS)
School of Law
Columbia, Mo. 65201
Requirements
Bachelor's + LSAT
Fall admission only
Application by March 31
Tuition
$460—residents
$920—nonresidents
Other Expenses
Room and board—$940

Books and supplies—$125

Missouri, University of,
Kansas City
(ABA, AALS)
School of Law
5100 Rockhill Rd.
Kansas City, Mo. 64110
Degree—J.D. + LL.M.
(Day–Eve)
Requirements
90 semester hours or
bachelor's + LSAT-
LSDAS
Fall admission only
Tuition
$800—residents
$1,700—nonresidents
Other Expenses
Room, board—$1,800

Montana, University of
(ABA, AALS)
School of Law
Missoula, Mont. 59801
Degree—J.D.
Requirements
Bachelor's + LSAT
Fall admission only
Application by May 1
Tuition
$426—residents
$1,293—nonresidents
Other Expenses
Books—approx. $150

Nebraska, University of
(ABA, AALS)

College of Law
Lincoln, Nebr. 68508
Degree—J.D.
Requirements
    Several undergraduate
        degree options +
        LSAT-LSDAS
    Applications accepted 1
        year prior to intended
        entrance date
Tuition
    $535—residents
    $1,261—nonresidents
Other Expenses
    Housing—approx. $1,000
    Books, supplies—approx.
        $150

New England School of Law
    (ABA)
47 Mt. Vernon St.
Boston, Mass. 02138
Degree—J.D. (Day–Eve)
Requirements
    Bachelor's + LSAT-
        LSDAS + 2 recom-
        mendations
    Application by April 1
Tuition
    $1,500

New Mexico, University of
    (ABA, AALS)
School of Law
Albuquerque, N. Mex. 87106
Degree—J.D.

Requirements
    Bachelor's + LSAT-
        LSDAS
Fall admission only
Application by April 15
Tuition
    $454—residents
    $1,248—nonresidents
Other Expenses
    Living, etc.—approx.
        $2,200
Percent Women Students
    17%

New York Law School
    (ABA, BRSNY)
57 Worth St.
New York, N.Y. 10013
Degree—J.D. (Day–Eve) +
    Special Programs
Requirements
    Bachelor's + LSAT-
        LSDAS
    Fall admission only
Tuition
    $1,600
Percent Women Students
    20% and increasing

New York University
    (ABA, AALS, BRSNY)
School of Law
Washington Square
New York, N.Y. 10003
Degree—J.D. + J.D.-
    M.B.A. + J.D.-Pub Ad-
    min. + J.S.D. +M.C.J.
    + Special Programs

Requirements
Bachelor's + LSAT-
LSDAS
Sept. admission only
Tuition
$2,600
Other Expenses
Room and board—
average $1,800
Books and misc.—$500
Percent Women Students
Approx. 30% in freshman
class

New York, State Univ. of,
Buffalo
(ABA, AALS)
School of Law
77 W. Eagle St.
Buffalo, N.Y. 14202
Degree—J.D. + Special
Programs
Requirements
Bachelor's + LSAT-
LSDAS
Fall admission only
Application by Feb. 15
Tuition
$1,600—residents
$2,000—nonresidents
Other Expenses
Room, board—approx.
$2,200
Percent Women Students
16% and increasing

North Carolina, University of
(ABA, AALS)

School of Law
Chapel Hill, N.C. 27514
Degree—J.D. + J.D.-
M.R.P. + J.D.-M.B.A.
Requirements
Bachelor's + LSAT-
LSDAS
Fall admission only
Application by March 31
Tuition
$420—residents
$2,000—nonresidents
Other Expenses
Housing—up to approx.
$700
Percent Women Students
10% and increasing

North Carolina Central
University
(ABA)
School of Law
Durham, N.C. 27707
Degree—J.D.
Requirements
3 years or 90 semester
hours + LSAT
Fall admission only
Application by March 1
Tuition
$1,227—residents
$2,827—nonresidents
Percent Women Students
25%

North Dakota, University of
(ABA, AALS)
School of Law

Grand Forks, N.D. 58201
Degree—J.D.
Requirements
 Bachelor's + LSAT-
  LSDAS
 Fall admission only
 Application by April 15
Tuition
 $464—resident
 $1,192—nonresident
Other Expenses
 Fees—approx. $100
 Books—approx. $130

Northeastern University
 (ABA, AALS)
School of Law
400 Huntington Ave.
Boston, Mass. 02115
Degree—J.D. (on coopera-
 tive plan, 1 year in law
 office before graduation)
Requirements
 Bachelor's + LSAT-
  LSDAS
 Application by March 1
Tuition
 $2,025—first year; books
  —approx. $150; $1,350
  —upper-class years;
  fees—approx. $150

Northern Kentucky State
 College
 (ABA)
Salmon P. Chase College of
 Law
1401 Dixie Highway

Covington, Ky. 41011
Degree—J.D. (Eve only)
Requirements
 Bachelor's + LSAT
 Fall admission only
 Application by March 1
Tuition
 $956—residents
 $1,056—nonresidents
Other Expenses
 Room, board—approx.
  $3,600

Northwestern University
 (ABA, AALS)
School of Law
357 E. Chicago Ave.
Chicago, Ill. 60611
Degree—J.D.
Requirements
 Bachelor's + LSAT-
  LSDAS
 Fall admission only
 Application by March 31
Tuition
 $2,800
Other Expenses
 $2,250 average

Notre Dame, University of
 (ABA, AALS)
Law School
Notre Dame, Ind. 46556
Degree—J.D. + J.D.-
 M.B.A + J.D.-M.Th. +
 J.D.-M.S.-E.H.E.
Requirements
 Bachelor's + LSAT

Fall admission only
Application by April 1
Tuition
$2,415
Other Expenses
Room, board—approx.
$1,200
Books, supplies, fees—
$250
Percent Women Students
Approx. 14% and increasing

Ohio Northern University
(ABA, AALS, State)
College of Law
Ada, Ohio 45810
Degree—J.D.
Requirements
Bachelor's + LSAT-
LSDAS
Fall admission only
Tuition
$2,016
Other Expenses
Room, board—approx.
$1,500

Ohio State University
(ABA, AALS, State)
College of Law
190 N. Oval Drive
Columbus, Ohio 43210
Degree—J.D.
Requirements
Bachelor's + LSAT
Fall admission only
Application by April

Tuition
$900—residents
$1,950—nonresidents
Other Expenses
Room, board—approx.
$2,200

Oklahoma, University of
(ABA, AALS)
College of Law
630 Parrington Oval
Norman, Okla. 73069
Degree—J.D.
Requirements
Bachelor's + LSAT-
LSDAS
Fall admission only
Application by April 15
Tuition
$510—residents
$1,260—nonresidents
Other Expenses
Room, board—approx.
$1,000

Oklahoma City University
(ABA)
Oklahoma City, Okla. 73106
Degree—J.D. (Eve only)
Requirements
Bachelor's + LSAT-
LSDAS
Fall admission only
Tuition
$1,260
Other Expenses
Room, board—approx.
$1,000

Oregon, University of
  (ABA, AALS)
School of Law
Eugene, Oreg. 97403
Degree—J.D.
Requirements
  Bachelor's + LSAT-
    LSDAS
  Fall admission only
  Application by April 1
Tuition
  $690
Other Expenses
  Room, board—$1,500
  Books and supplies—$200
Percent Women Students
  Approx. 9%

Pacific, University of the
  (ABA, State)
McGeorge School of Law
3200 Fifth Ave.
Sacramento, Calif. 95817
Degree—J.D. (Day–Eve)
Requirements
  Bachelor's + LSAT
  Fall admission only
Tuition
  $1,890
Other Expenses
  Room and board—$1,800
  Books and supplies—$150

Pennsylvania, University of
  (ABA, AALS)
Law School
3400 Chestnut St.
Philadelphia, Pa. 19104

Degree—J.D. + LL.M. +
  LL.C.M. + J.S.D.
Requirements
  Bachelor's + LSAT-
    LSDAS
  Fall admission only
  Application by March 1
Tuition
  $2,900
Other Expenses
  General fee—$150; books
    —$180
  Room and board—$1,530

Pepperdine University
  (ABA, State)
School of Law
12345 Westminster Ave.
Santa Ana, Calif. 92703
Degree—J.D. (Day–Eve)
Requirements
  Bachelor's + LSAT-
    LSDAS
  Fall admission only
  Application by May 1
Tuition
  Approx. $2,000
Other Expenses
  Books, supplies—approx.
    $150

Pittsburgh, University of
  (ABA, AALS)
School of Law
Pittsburgh, Pa. 15213
Degree—J.D.
Requirements

Bachelor's + LSAT-
 LSDAS
Fall admission only
Tuition
 $1,050—residents
 $2,040—nonresidents
Other Expenses
 Dormitory—$570

Richmond, University of
 (ABA, AALS, BRSNY,
 State)
T. C. Williams School of Law
Richmond, Va. 23173
Degree—J.D.
Requirements
 Bachelor's + LSAT-
 LSDAS + recommen-
 dations
 Fall admission only
 Application by Oct. 15
Tuition
 $2,025
Other Expenses
 Room and board—$1,050
 Books—approx. $125

Rutgers, State University of
 N.J.
 (ABA, AALS)
School of Law
311 N. 5th St.
Camden, N.J. 08102
Degree—J.D.
Requirements
 Bachelor's + LSAT-
 LSDAS
 Fall admission only

Tuition
 $580

Rutgers, State University of
 N.J.
 (ABA, AALS, BRSNY)
School of Law
180 University Ave.
Newark, N.J. 07102
Degree—J.D. + J.D.-M.A.
Requirements
 Bachelor's + LSAT-
 LSDAS
 Application by April 1
Tuition
 $500
Other Expenses
 Room, board—approx.
 $2,500
 Books—$120; fees—$80

St. John's University
 (ABA, AALS, BRSNY)
School of Law
Grand Central and Utopia
 Parkways
Jamaica, N.Y. 11439
Degree—J.D. (Day–Eve)
Requirements
 Bachelor's + LSAT-
 LSDAS
 Application by May 1
 (fall); Dec. 1 (spring)
Tuition
 $2,200

St. Louis University
 (ABA, AALS)

School of Law
3642 Lindell Blvd.
St. Louis, Mo. 63108
Requirements
    Bachelor's + LSAT-
        LSDAS
    Fall admission only
Tuition
    $2,050
Other Expenses
    Room, board—approx.
        $1,200

St. Mary's University
    (ABA, AALS, State)
School of Law
2700 Cincinnati Ave.
San Antonio, Tex. 78284
Degree—J.D.
Requirements
    Bachelor's + LSAT-
        LSDAS + two recom-
        mendations
Tuition
    $1,650
Other Expenses
    Lodging—to $600
Percent Women Students
    Approx. 6%

Samford University
    (ABA, AALS, BRSNY)
Cumberland School of Law
800 Lakeshore Drive
Birmingham, Ala. 35209
Degree—J.D. (Day–Eve),
    J.D.-M.B.A. + J.D.-M.A.

Requirements
    Bachelor's + LSAT
    Fall or spring admission
Tuition
    $1,320

San Diego, University of
    (ABA, AALS, State)
School of Law
Alcala Park
San Diego, Calif. 92110
Degree—J.D. (Day–Eve)
Requirements
    Bachelor's + LSAT-
        LSDAS
    Fall admission only
    Application by March 1
Tuition
    $1,700
Other Expenses
    Books—approx. $150

San Francisco, University of
    (ABA, AALS, BRSNY)
School of Law
San Francisco, Calif. 94117
Degree—J.D. (Day–Part
    Eve)
Requirements
    Bachelor's + LSAT-
        LSDAS
    Fall admission only
    Application by March 1
Tuition
    $1,935
Percent Women Students
    Almost 20%

Santa Clara, University of
(ABA, AALS)
School of Law
Santa Clara, Calif. 95053
Degree—J.D. (Day–Eve)
Requirements
Bachelor's + LSAT-
LSDAS
Application by Feb.
Tuition
$2,070
Other Expenses
Room, board, books—
$2,000

Seton Hall University
(ABA, AALS, State)
School of Law
40 Clinton St.
Newark, N.J. 07102
Degree—J.D. (Day–Eve)
Requirements
Bachelor's + LSAT-
LSDAS
Fall admission only
Application by Feb.
Tuition
$1,625

South Carolina, University of
(ABA, AALS)
School of Law
1515 Green Street
Columbia, S.C. 29208
Degree—J.D.
Requirements
Bachelor's + LSAT
Fall admission only

Application by May 1
Tuition
$570—residents
$1,280—nonresidents
Other Expenses
Room, board—up to
$1,020
Various plans available

South Dakota, University of
(ABA, AALS)
School of Law
Vermillion, S. Dak. 57069
Degree—J.D.
Requirements
Bachelor's + LSAT-
LSDAS
Application by March 1
Tuition
$648—residents
$1,396—nonresidents
Other Expenses
Fees—approx. $150;
books—$150
Room, board—approx.
$1,000

South Texas College of Law
(ABA, State)
1220 Polk Avenue
Houston, Tex. 77002
Degree—J.D. (Eve. only)
Requirements
Bachelor's + LSAT
Tuition
$1,100
Other Expenses
Books—approx. $225

Southern University
  (ABA)
Southern Branch Post Office
Baton Rouge, La. 70813
Degree—J.D.
Requirements
  Bachelor's + LSAT
  Application by May 15
Tuition
  Free for residents
  $600—nonresidents
Other Expenses
  Fees—$300

Southern California,
  University of
  (ABA, AALS)
Law Center
University Park
Los Angeles, Calif. 90007
Degree—J.D. + LL.M. +
  Special Programs
Requirements
  Bachelor's + LSAT-
    LSDAS
  Application by April 1
Tuition
  $2,840
  Fees—$60
Other Expenses
  Room and board—$1,330

Southern Methodist
  University
  (ABA, AALS)
School of Law
Dallas, Tex. 75222

Degree—J.D. + LL.M. +
  J.S.D. + M.C.L.
Requirements
  Bachelor's + LSAT-
    LSDAS
  Fall admission only
  Application by March 1
Tuition
  $2,000
Other Expenses
  Room and board—$1,200

Southwestern University
  (ABA, State)
School of Law
1121 S. Hill St.
Los Angeles, Calif. 90015
Degree—J.D. (Day–Eve)
Requirements
  Bachelor's* + LSAT-
    LSDAS
  Application by June
  Fall admission only
Tuition
  Approx. $1,300
Other Expenses
  Books and supplies—$200

Stanford University
  (ABA, AALS)
School of Law
Stanford, Calif. 94305
Degree—J.D. + J.M. +
  J.S.D. + J.S.M.
Requirements
  Bachelor's + LSAT-
    LSDAS
  Fall admission only

Application by Jan. 1
Tuition
  $2,850
Other Expenses
  Room, board—approx.
    $1,400
  Books, supplies—approx.
    $200

Stetson University
  (ABA, AALS)
College of Law
St. Petersburg, Fla. 33707
Degree—J.D.
Requirements
  Bachelor's +LSAT-
    LSDAS
Tuition
  $2,000
Other Expenses
  Fees—approx. $75
  Room—approx. $500

Suffolk University
  (ABA)
41 Temple St.
Boston, Mass. 02114
Degree—J.D. (Day–Eve)
Requirements
  Bachelor's + LSAT
  Fall admission only
  Application by Feb. 15
Tuition
  $1,500

Syracuse University
  (ABA, AALS, BRSNY)
College of Law
Syracuse, N.Y. 13210

Degree—J.D. + Special
  Programs
Requirements
  Bachelor's + LSAT
  Fall admission only
Tuition
  $2,740

Temple University
  (ABA, AALS)
School of Law
1715 N. Broad St.
Philadelphia, Pa. 19122
Degree—J.D. (Day–Eve) +
  LL.M.
Requirements
  Bachelor's + LSAT-
    LSDAS
  Fall admission only
  Application by March 1
Tuition
  $970—residents
  $1,870—nonresidents
Other Expenses
  Room, board—approx.
    $1,200
  Books, supplies—$200
Percent Women Students
  12% and increasing

Tennessee, University of
  (ABA, AALS)
College of Law
Knoxville, Tenn. 37916
Degree—J.D
Requirements
  Bachelor's + LSAT-
    LSDAS

Summer and fall admission
Application by March 15
Tuition
$384—residents
$1,104—nonresidents
Other Expenses
Room, board, books—
approx. $1,800

Texas, University of
(ABA, AALS)
School of Law
2500 Red River St.
Austin, Tex. 78705
Degree—J.D. + LL.M. +
M.C.J.
Requirements
Bachelor's + LSAT-
LSDAS
Application by March 1
Tuition
$260—residents
$1,260—nonresidents
Other Expenses
Living—approx. $2,000

Texas Tech. University
(ABA, AALS, State)
School of Law
Box 4030
Lubbock, Tex. 79409
Degree—J.D.
Requirements
Bachelor's + LSAT-
LSDAS
Fall admission only
Application by March 1

Tuition
$228—residents
$1,380—nonresidents
Other Expenses
Living—approx. $2,100
Books, supplies—approx.
$150
Percent Women Students
7%

Toledo, University of
(ABA, AALS, State)
College of Law
Toledo, Ohio 43606
Degree—J.D. (Part Day–
Eve)
Requirements
Bachelor's + LSAT-
LSDAS
Application by April 1
Tuition
$1,035—residents
$2,190—nonresidents
Other Expenses
Living—approx. $2,000

Tulane University
(ABA, AALS)
School of Law
New Orleans, La. 70118
Degree—J.D. + LL.M. +
M.C.L. + D.J.S.
Requirements
96 semester hours +
LSAT-LSDAS
Fall admission only
Application by May 15
Tuition
$2,450

Other Expenses
Room, board—approx.
$1,050

Tulsa, University of
(ABA, AALS)
College of Law
3120 E. Fourth Place
Tulsa, Okla. 74104
Degree—J.D. (Day–Eve)
Requirements
Bachelor's + LSAT-
LSDAS
Tuition
$1,700
Other Expenses
$1,350
Books, supplies—approx.
$200

Utah, University of
(ABA, AALS)
College of Law
Salt Lake City, Utah 84112
Degree—J.D.
Requirements
Bachelor's + LSAT-
LSDAS
Fall admission only
Application by April 1
Tuition
$520—residents
$1,060—nonresidents
Other Expenses
Books, supplies—average
$500

Valparaiso University
(ABA, AALS)

School of Law
Valparaiso, Ind. 46383
Degree—J.D.
Requirements
Bachelor's + LSAT-
LSDAS
Fall admission only
Tuition
$2,090

Vanderbilt University
(ABA, AALS)
School of Law
Nashville, Tenn. 37240
Degree—J.D.
Requirements
Bachelor's +LSAT-
LSDAS
Fall admission only
Application by Feb. 1
Tuition
$2,400
Percent Women Students
6% and increasing

Villanova University
(ABA, AALS)
School of Law
Villanova, Pa. 19085
Degree—J.D.
Requirements
Bachelor's +LSAT
Tuition
$1,825
Other Expenses
Room and board—$1,200

Virginia, University of
(ABA, AALS)

School of Law
Charlottesville, Va. 22901
Degree—J.D. + several
    combined degrees M.A.-
    J.D. and M.B.A.-J.D.
Requirements
    Bachelor's +LSAT-
    LSDAS
    Fall admission only
Application by Feb. 1
Tuition
    $714—residents
    $1,639—nonresidents
Other Expenses
    Approx. $1,850
Percent Women Students
    Approx. 7%

Wake Forest University
    (ABA, AALS, State)
School of Law
Winston-Salem, N.C. 27109
Degree—J.D.
Requirements
    Bachelor's + LSAT-
    LSDAS
    Application by Feb. 1
Tuition
    $1,500
    Fees—$90
Other Expenses
    Room, board—approx.
    $1,000
    Books—approx. $150

Washburn University of
    Topeka
    (ABA, AALS)

School of Law
    Topeka, Kans. 66621
Degree—J.D. (Day–Eve)
Requirements
    Bachelor's + LSAT-
    LSDAS
    Application by March 15
    Admission in fall only
Tuition
    $925
Percent Women Students
    Approx. 4% and increas-
    ing

Washington, University of
    (ABA, AALS)
School of Law
Seattle, Wash. 98195
Degree—J.D. + LL.M. +
    Ph.D. + J.D.-M.B.A.
Requirements
    Bachelor's + LSAT-
    LSDAS + recommen-
    dations
    Fall admission only
    Application by Feb. 1
Tuition
    $624—residents
    $1,641—nonresidents
Other Expenses
    $2,500
Percent Women Students
    Over 25%

Washington and Lee Univer-
    sity
    (ABA, AALS)
School of Law

Lexington, Va. 24450
Degree—J.D.
Requirements
   Bachelor's + LSAT +
      recommendations
   Fall admission only
   Application by Feb. 1
Tuition
   $1,900
Other Expenses
   Room and board—$1,040

Washington University
   (ABA, AALS)
School of Law
St. Louis, Mo. 63130
Degree—J.D. + J.S.D. +
   LL.M. + Special Pro-
   grams
Requirements
   Bachelor's + LSAT-
      LSDAS
   Suggest fall entrance
Tuition
   $2,600
Other Expenses
   Room, board, books—
      over $2,000
Percent Women Students
   About 15%

Wayne State University
   (ABA, AALS)
Law School
468 W. Ferry Ave.
Detroit, Mich. 48202
Degree—J.D. (Day–Eve) +
   LL.M. (in Taxation,

Labor Relations and
   Corporate Planning)
Requirements
   Bachelor's + LSAT-
      LSDAS
   Fall admission only
   Application by April 15
Tuition
   $884—residents
   $1,800—nonresidents
Other Expenses
   Living—$3,000

West Virginia University
   (ABA, AALS)
College of Law
1530 University Ave.
Morgantown, W. Va. 26505
Degree—J.D.
Requirements
   Bachelor's + LSAT-
      LSDAS
   Fall admission only
   Application by March 1
Tuition
   $322—residents
   $972—nonresidents
Other Expenses
   Room and board—$1,600
   Books and supplies—$225

Willamette University
   (ABA, AALS)
Salem, Oreg. 97301
Degree—J.D.
Requirements
   Bachelor's + LSAT-
      LSDAS

Application by April 2
Tuition
  $1,940
  Fees—$54
Other Expenses
  Room, board—approx.
    $1,000
Percent Women Students
  Approx. 7% and increas-
    ing

William and Mary, College of
  (ABA, AALS)
Marshall-Whythe School of
  Law
Williamsburg, Va. 23185
Degree—J.D. + M.L.T.
Requirements
  Bachelor's + LSAT
  Application by Feb. 15
Tuition
  $706—residents
  $1,776—nonresidents
Other Expenses
  Room, board—approx.
    $1,600

William Mitchell College of
  Law
  (ABA)
St. Paul, Minn. 55105
Degree—J.D. (Eve only)
Requirements
  Bachelor's + LSAT
  Fall admission only
Tuition
  $950

Other Expenses
  Books—approx. $150
Percent Women Students
  About 5%

Wisconsin, University of
  (ABA, AALS)
Law School
Madison, Wis. 53706
Degree—J.D. + LL.M +
  J.S.D.
Requirements
  Bachelor's + LSAT-
    LSDAS
  Fall admission only
  Application by Feb. 15
Tuition
  $640—residents
  $2,200—nonresidents
Other Expenses
  Living—$2,100
Percent Women Students
  11% and increasing

Wyoming, University of
  (ABA, AALS)
University Station
Laramie, Wyo. 82070
Degree—J.D.
Requirements
  Bachelor's + LSAT-
    LSDAS
  Application by March 1
Tuition
  $410—residents
  $1,376—nonresidents
Other Expenses
  Average $2,000

Percent Women Students
10%

Yale University
(ABA, AALS)
Law School
New Haven, Conn. 06520
Degree—J.D. + LL.M. +
J.S.D. +D.C.L. + J.D.-
M.A.
Requirements

Bachelor's + LSAT +
recommendations
Fall admission only
Application by Feb. 1
Tuition
$3,100
Other Expenses
Room, board—approx.
$2,350
Percent Women Students
Approx. 18%

Index